Teach Your Child to Read

Kerry Dickinson

FOR SEAN,
THANK YOU FOR ALWAYS PUSHING ME TO DO MORE

.

TEACH YOUR CHILD TO READ:
AN EASY-TO-READ GUIDEBOOK ON HOW TO TEACH YOUR CHILD TO READ AT HOME

CONTENTS

1   Introduction   1

2   What is Phonics and Why is it taught?   2

3   Pre-Reading   5

4   Early Reading   8

5   Developing Reading   12

6   Developing Skills to Read Words Quickly   13

7   Learning to Read Unfamiliar Words   14

8   Becoming a Fluent Reader   18

9   The Phonics Screening   20

10 Reading Difficulties   21

11 Pre-Reading Activities   26

12 Early Reading Activities   35

13 Activities for Reading   41

14 Reading Material   42

15 Letter, Sound Recognition   45

16 Reading Manipulatives   47

17 Reading Tricky Words   52

18 Word reading   54

19	Reading Harder Words	59
20	Caption and Sentence Reading	62
21	Reading Strategies	63
22	Reading Fluency	64
23	Reading Comprehension	65
24	Useful Resources	67
25	Sound Lists	69
26	Word Lists	72
27	Word Lists in Sound Families	78
28	Captions and Sentences	93
29	Printables	98
	Glossary	100
	References and Picture Acknowledgements	103
	About the Author	105

1
INTRODUCTION

For many years I taught reading in the classroom, but I felt like it wasn't enough so I became involved in mentoring student teachers and yet that still wasn't enough. I realised there was still such extreme need and that I needed to extend the scope of my classroom. I thought carefully about how children learn to read and concluded that the person who has the greatest impact on a child's life and academics and can affect the most change is not a teacher, it's the parent.

I recognised that to affect real change I would need to teach parents to teach reading. Children start learning to read before birth through listening to their parents talk, read and sing. Reading is a form of communication and connection and the best teachers of this are parents. Reading is one of the most important things a child will ever learn as without the ability to read your child will struggle to learn anything else.

This book is written in the United Kingdom and uses the 2014 Primary National Curriculum in England as the framework within which the children are taught. The principles are the same worldwide, but the age the children learn to read and write may differ.

There are many excellent Phonics, spelling and reading products and programmes on the market; this is not one of those. This is a practical book for parents who would like more knowledge and ideas on how to teach their children to read in a fun and natural way.

This book begins with some key terminology so that you can confidently converse with educationalists about your child's progress. The teaching of reading is divided into six phases, in each phase, there is an explanation of the critical elements and advice on helping your child in that phase. There is also a general outline of some learning difficulties and then activities to engage your child in reading.

At the end of the book are various word lists that can be used as reference material. This book is for busy parents, some of the ideas are quick and easy, and some require a little more preparation. Find the activities that you enjoy doing with your child and focus on those. Children learn more when they are enjoying themselves, so be creative, be yourself and have fun.

2
WHAT IS PHONICS AND WHY IS IT TAUGHT?

Children are taught to read using phonics because research has found that this is the best way for most children to learn to read. However, some children will find learning to read this way difficult; these children are known as sight readers, and they learn how to read whole words and memorise those words. Traditionally children were taught to read whole words; however, the brain can only hold a finite number of whole words. Children also had a limited number of ways to read unfamiliar words.

Children are given strategies to read unfamiliar words from the start with Phonics, they are taught the structure and rules of words and can use this knowledge to read any word, significantly increasing their reading ability. Children are taught the sounds in quick succession and start reading early in the process, and this increases their confidence in their capabilities and helps build a love of reading. This book is primarily focused on teaching reading using phonics.

All language and text activities help children learn to read; however, formal teaching of reading starts in the Reception Year when the child is four years old. They learn Phonics daily in a sequential incremental manner. Children are taught to recognise and blend sounds in English from left to right in an interactive multi-sensory manner.

English is a relatively new language and comprises various root languages, including German, French, Greek, Saxon, and Latin. It is challenging for children to learn to read in English as many of the spellings have been retained from the original languages. Reading is an essential skill that dictates a child's future academic success.

We speak using sounds or phonemes, we spell using graphemes, and we read by linking phonemes and graphemes together in a meaningful way. Phonics is a method of teaching spelling and reading by linking sounds to the letters that represent those sounds. The teaching of Phonics starts in the early years and does not end; there are always new rules to learn or words to read.

Sounds joined together when spoken form words; we call these sounds phonemes. In the word **bat,** there are three sounds joined together to make the word. The sound **b** is at the beginning of the word, **a** in the middle and **t** at the end of the word, so, **bat** has three sounds **b-a-t**, it has three phonemes.

Teach children to listen to the individual sounds in words. A child must recognise a letter (or group of letters), link those letters with sounds, and then join the sounds to read a word; dividing a word into its component sounds is called segmenting. Blending is when you say segmented sounds together to form a word. When reading the word **sheep,** the child will say the sounds **sh-ee-p** then join the sounds together to read the word **sheep.**

When we push sounds together to read a word, it called blending.

When children read, they:
- Read from left to right while converting letters to sounds.
- Blend the sounds.
- Pronounce the word.

When a child writes a word, they start with the whole word, and then they break the word into separate sounds. The child says the word **chip,** then sounds it out as **ch-i-p**; as they sound it out, they write down the letter representations for those sounds.

When children spell, they:
- Say the word.
- Identify the sounds from the beginning to the end.
- Write down the letter sounds from left to right.

A grapheme is a letter or group of letters that represent a sound. Graphemes can consist of one to four letters. A grapheme that has one letter is called a graph. In the word **cat**, there are three phonemes because there are three sounds. **Cat** has three sounds, and three graphemes as the number of graphemes equal the number of phonemes; in the word **cat,** each grapheme is called a graph as they have only one letter.

In the word **paid**, there are four letters but three sounds and three spelling choices. The number of graphemes equals the number of phonemes. The graph **p** represents the initial sound, the graph **d** is the final sound, and the middle sound is made with two letters together to form the **ai** sound. Two letters together that make one sound is called a digraph.

A trigraph is a spelling choice formed by joining three letters together to make one sound. In the word **patch** there are three sounds. The graph **p** represents the first sound, the middle sound is the graph **a**, and the final sound **tch**, is formed using three letters, **tch** is a trigraph.

A four-letter spelling choice is called a quadgraph. Quadgraphs are rare and seldom need to be taught, but it is good to be able to identify and explain them. The word **eight** has two sounds; the initial sound is the quadgraph **eigh**, and the graph **t** represents the final sound. In Phase Five, sounds that are spelt differently are called alternate spellings. For example, the **ai** sound can be spelt as ai in the word **train**, **a-e** in the word **cake**, **a** in **baby**, **ea** in **great**, **ey** in

grey or **ay** in **play**.

The English alphabet consists of twenty-six letters; however, spoken English comprises forty-four or forty-six sounds depending on your language expert and regional accent. As a result, some sounds are created using a combination of letters known as digraphs, trigraphs and quadgraphs. The following sounds are the generally agreed upon sounds in the English language, along with the most common graphemes for each phoneme. The digraph **qu** is two separate sounds, but we teach it as one as it is challenging for young children to understand. The 'graph' **x** is also two distinct sounds, but we teach it as one sound to avoid confusion.

The Sounds in The English Language

Consonant Sounds	b	bird	Short Vowel Sounds	a	apple
	c/k	cat/key		e	egg
	d	dog		i	ink
	f	fish		o	orange
	g	goat		u	umbrella
	h	hat		oo	book
	j	jet	Long Vowel Sounds	ai	rain
	l	leaf		ee	tree
	m	mat		ie	tie
	n	nose		oa	oats
	p	pet		u-e	cube
	qu	queen		oo	spoon
	r	rat		oi	boil
	s	socks		ow	cow
	t	tap	Controlled R Vowel	ar	car
	v	vet	sounds	ir	girl
	w	wet		or	order
	x	box		air	chair
	y	yellow		ear	beard
	z	zebra		ure	cure
	s	treasure			
Consonant Digraphs	sh	ship			
	ch	chip			
	th	feather			
	th	tooth			
	ng	king			

3
PRE-READING

The skills and experiences children need to become proficient readers are called pre-reading and writing skills and are referred to as Phase One. Some of these activities may seem unrelated to reading but they all develop the child's listening, speaking and communication skills. It is important to continue these activities after children have learnt to read to embed them and foster a love of reading.

Children must enjoy books and have positive experiences around reading before learning to read. They need to read with their parents, listen to stories, go on trips to book shops and the local library, and explore books independently. All these activities inspire a child to want to learn to read.

There is a huge variety of excellent children's literature to choose from, fairy tales or traditional tales as they are now called, are valuable for teaching the structure of stories. Religious stories help children learn shared values within a community and develop a better understanding of their faith. While stories from other religions develop a child's tolerance and understanding of different belief systems.

When children listen to books that contain rhyming words, they begin to recognise similarities and differences in words. Children love to join in with stories and may even predict the words in the story as they develop their understanding of rhyming words and expand their vocabularies.

Books containing alliterations highlight similarities and differences in sounds at the beginning of words. When you read these books, the children can think of other words that also start with the same sound and continue to deepen their knowledge of the sounds that make up words and the similarities and differences between words. Good picture books grab children's attention, they have interesting characters, excellent artwork, a good storyline, and twists in the tale. When reading picture books, remember to point to the text on the page as you read as this helps children to associate the words they can hear with the print on the page.

Books without text are also important, with these books make up the story as they go along, talk about setting, characters and actions. Storytelling is an ancient tradition going back thousands of years. These stories can be told without the aid of a book and will foster a child's love of stories and develop their imagination and understanding of plot. Children can contribute to the stories and decide on the characters, setting, twists in the tale or the ending.

Audiobooks improve children's listening skills. Some audiobooks come with picture books so that the child can look at the pictures while listening to the story, these are particularly useful for younger children or children who struggle to focus without a visual aid. Listening to stories is a skill that takes time to develop but significantly impacts on a child's listening abilities. You may need to begin this activity with the aid of a book. Audiobooks are also a great alternative to tablets in the car.

Create a word rich environment, by labelling everything, including the furniture. Point out words and sentences when you are out and model reading. Your child will soon start to read and recognise familiar words and symbols.

Good communication skills are vital to learning to read and write and adults should model speaking, listening, and turn-taking skills. Talk to children in complete sentences, use good vocabulary and avoid any baby language. Insist that children must use the right words for objects. Repeat words or sentences back to children correctly. For example, if your child says: "The doggy is black." Then say: "Yes, I agree the **dog** is black."

If the child is in the habit of pointing at objects rather than using the words, then teach them the vocabulary and gently encourage them to vocally request things. For example, if you ask what they would like to play with and they point at the teddy bear then you can say: "Would you like the teddy bear? This is called a teddy bear. Can you say teddy bear?" This way the child hears the phrase several times and hopefully says the word at least once and begins to develop both receptive and expressive vocabulary. Give your child plenty of time to speak, as sometimes it takes a child time to think of the words they need and try not to complete their sentences for them or answer questions for them. Children learn through play; they are constantly communicating while playing and should be allowed as much time as possible for free play. Free play is not structured, planned or adult led, it is child initiated, open ended and engaging. Children should not be continuously entertained as this limits their ability to think of play ideas for themselves and in turn limits their imagination.

In Phase One, it is essential to develop a child's awareness of the sounds in their environment. Take your child for a listening walk, then have them stop and listen to what they can hear in the world around them. Use plenty of drama and intrigue when saying: "What can you hear?" The child then identifies what they have heard, a siren of a passing police car, an aeroplane flying overhead, or a dog barking in the distance and goes on to explain if it is near or far and maybe even makes up a story around what they have heard. Encourage them to reproduce the sounds they can hear; this is lots of fun when playing pretend or dressing up. They can make siren noises, animal noises, weather noises or make up voices to accompany the characters in their play.

Playing instruments and music develops a child's awareness of sounds and their listening skills. Children need these skills to hear the sounds in words. Have noise makers available for free play and incorporate them into their lives. Instruments can be played loudly, softly, fast, slow, or simply just for fun. Have your child describe what they can hear while playing instruments.

Nursery Rhymes introduce children to new vocabulary, speech patterns, rhythm, and rhyme. They also develop memory and are an essential part of creating a cultural identity. You can use body percussion while singing, acting out or saying rhymes to help your child better remember the rhymes and develop their fine and gross motor skills. One rhyme can be done several different ways, you are only limited to your imagination For example, with the Rhyme Insy Winsy Spider, the rhyme can be said loudly, softly, quickly, slowly or in different voices. You can take turns saying the different phrases in the rhyme or perform it as a round. You can paint spider and web pictures, go on a spider hunt or research spiders. All these activities develop the child's language, phonics, and vocabulary skills.

It is fun as the parent to play with words and sounds; make up silly sounds or words, and you're your child copy, make up silly rhymes or words or play word association games like, "I went to the zoo, and I saw…"

You can model sound talking (sounding out words) and blending words throughout the day, 'Please put away your **b-a-g, bag**.' After a while, your child will naturally begin hearing and blending the words themselves. You can then say: "Put away your b-a-g…" and they can say "bag!" Only sound out the last word in the sentence; otherwise, it becomes confusing for young children. Avoid sounding out words with two consonants next to each, as these will be hard for the children to hear.

At this stage, your child has not been formally introduced to any letters or told what sounds these letters represent. This phase is about developing a child's sound awareness through oral games with words and sounds.

4
EARLY READING

During the pre-reading phase, or Phase One, the vocabulary of language: words, letters, sentences, sounds, letter names were all used interchangeably. In Phase Two, or early reading phase, your child starts to distinguish between these terms and to understand the concept of words. Children begin to move from oral segmenting and blending activities to segmenting and blending with letters. They start to separate sentences into words, then words into syllables and lastly, words into sounds when writing and blending sounds into words and words into sentences when reading. It is a magical time for both you and your child.

Your child learns to recognise a letter (or group of letters) and to link those letters with sounds to read a word, they then join (or blend) all the sounds in the word together. Children who have had a lot of practice with orally blending sounds find it easier to blend letters and read words.

At school, children learn nineteen different sounds and their letter representations. They also learn that sometimes two letters make one sound. Do not approach these digraphs as something new or more complicated, simply different; children accept the idea and read the digraph **ll** as one sound and not as **l, l**.

The first stage in this process is learning the letter sounds. Begin by saying lots of words that begin with the new sound. Sing a song with the sound in it or tell a story containing words with the sound and have your child indicate, or do an action, when they hear the sound. Programmes such as *Jolly Phonics* encourage children to use actions for each sound; they have songs, stories, and activities suitable for teaching young children. An action linked to a sound can prompt a child when they are unsure of the sound. Show your child what the letter looks like and how to write the letter. Children usually hear the initial sounds clearly; they later develop the ability to hear final sounds and later sounds within words.

It is best to introduce the letter name alongside the letter sound. "This is the letter **s** (name), and it makes the sound **s** (sound)." That way, there is no confusion when another adult says the letter's name. However, the emphasis should be on the letter sound. Review the letter names when you practice saying the alphabet. Insist the children use the letter sounds when they are reading to sound out words.

Most phonics programmes teach the sounds for the letters **s, a, t, p, i** and **n** first as these letters can make many two and three-letter words. These letters are also dissimilar from each other visually and audibly and, therefore, the most straightforward for children to distinguish.

The letters **b** and **d** are in separate groups to reduce confusion.

Most consonant sounds can be said with an inflexion on the end, an inflexion is an "uh" sound; this extra sound is called a schwa. Pure sounds are the sounds that are said with as little a schwa as possible. When teaching your child Phonics, try to make pure sounds to allow your child to hear the correct sounds and blend the word correctly. The word **dog** can be sounded out as **duh-o-guh**; this results in the word **duhoguh**. However, when sounded out with pure sounds, the same word becomes **d-o-g** and can be blended to say **dog**.

Some children develop a habit of dragging out the sounds. Encourage your child to say the sounds quickly and crisply as this will best facilitate blending the sounds to form words. Children will be unable to hear the word being sounded out if each sound is dragged out.

When teaching children new sounds and their letter representations, have them watch you closely. For a voiced sound, they can feel the vibrations in their voice boxes by gently placing their hands on their throats while saying the sound. If the sound is unvoiced, they can put their hand in front of their mouths to feel the air escaping.

· **Voiced and unvoiced Sounds**

Voiced Sounds		Unvoiced Sounds	
r	rat	s	sun
v	van	f	fan
d	dog	k	kit
g	goat	t	tap
s	pleasure	p	pot
z	zebra	b	box
b	bat	ch	chip
j	jet	th	thin
th	feather	sh	ship
l	leg	h	hat
m	man		
n	net		
All the vowel sounds			

In the Early Reading Phase children learn single letter sounds and some consonant digraphs. They blend these to read words. Expose your child to the sounds in different positions in words. The **s** sound can be at the beginning of a word **(sun)**, in the middle **(loot)**, or at the end **(pots)**.

If your child can sound out the word and say the letter sounds but cannot blend them into a word, then say the sounds with your child repeatedly, getting slightly quicker each time until they hear and say the word. If the child takes too long to recognise and articulate the sounds, they may not hear the word, so they must identify the sounds quickly and blend them with a degree of speed.

That is why there is a lot of emphasis on using flashcards and games that require the child to recognise the sounds rapidly. Flashcards and oral blending practise should happen daily at this stage.

Blending skills need to be taught and modelled. At first, your child may need visual prompts like an action to recognise the letter sounds. Say the initial sound louder than the others when teaching your child to sound out and blend words; this helps them remember the initial sound. This is essential for a child that drops the initial sound when reading; they may say, **at** for **cat,** the child is blending but has either not heard or has forgotten the initial sound.

Words should be presented meaningfully within text or with pictures and not isolated on their own. Children start by reading VC (vowel, consonant) and CVC (consonant, vowel, consonant) words, as these are the most straightforward words for children to sound out and blend together.

Children also need to be introduced to the mechanics of reading, such as the fact that we read from left to right and a page from the top to bottom of a page. Show them that sounds joined together create words and words joined together sensibly make sentences. Point out the spaces that separate words in a sentence as well as capital letter at the beginning of sentences and full stops at the end of sentences. When reading to your child point to the words and show your child how to read from left to right and top to bottom.

Check that your child's reading books are matched to their reading ability. A book that is too easy does not give the child a chance to develop their skills, while a book that is too difficult may make the child feel defeated and want to give up. In the early stages of reading, there should not be too many words on each page. Most of the words should be decodable with a few familiar Tricky Words. There should also be lots of repetition; this builds confidence and gives the child an opportunity to revise new words.

Children are not expected to read every word in their books, they are guided through the book by you as an enthusiastic and encouraging adult. They can say the initial or final sound in the words or sound out and read only the words you know they have the phonemic knowledge to read. They could read words that have obvious picture clues like the word dog under the picture of a dog or look for specific sounds or words in the book.

Point at the words as they read and encouraged the child to do the same, this helps reinforce the relationship between printed and oral words, develops the habit of reading from left to right and strengthens the child's visual tracking skills.

Check your child's aural recognition and visual recognition. If you say the sounds **b-a-t,** the child should say the word **bat,** and if the child sees the word **rat,** they should sound it out **r-a-t** and read the word **rat.**

Phase Two Sounds

s	socks	a	apple	t	tap	p	pot
i	ink	n	nose	m	mouse	d	dog
g	goat	o	orange	c	cat	k	king
ck	duck	e	egg	u	umbrella	r	rat
h	hat	b	bat	f	fish	ff	muffin
l	leaf	ll	jelly	ss	hiss		

Segmenting is when a child breaks up a word into different sounds. The child says the word and then counts how many sounds they can hear on their fingers. For example, **rat, r-a-t, rat** has three sounds (phonemes). The child then writes each sound to form a word. CVC words are the easiest to sound out and write.

Teach your child to write from left to right and top to bottom and observe them when they are writing; the finished word may appear to have been written backwards but, the child may have written the sounds in order but from right to left. Left-handed children tend to do this more than right-handed children.

Play games where children need to identify the position of the sound in a word such as:
- Where is **t** sound in **tap?**
- Where is the **t** sound in **pot?**
- Where is the **tt** in **butter?**

Teach your child to read Tricky Words, these are commonly used words that are important for children to read to access simple texts but do not fall within the child's existing phonemic knowledge. Show your child the "tricky" part of the word and the decodable part; this makes the word easier to remember. For example, in the word **he,** the child knows the **h** sound and is shown that the letter **e** can make an **ee** sound. Tricky Words are also known as Common Exception Words. The Tricky Words in Phase Two are: **the, to, I, no, go** and **into.**

Early reading activities take place in the Reception Year. However, some children may still be working on this stage in Year One and even Year Two; if this is the case, please see the chapter on reading difficulties.

5
DEVELOPING READING

In Phase Three children learn the remaining letters of the alphabet and some digraphs and trigraphs, this phase is taught in Reception. Children find recognising digraphs and trigraphs in words difficult at first and will often sound out the word **rain** as **r-a-i-n** instead of as **r-ai-n**. However, most children will start seeing and reading digraphs and trigraphs in words with a bit of time and practice.

Children are also exposed to decodable polysyllabic words so that they do not develop a fear or avoidance of "Big words." Compound words are the most accessible polysyllabic words for children to read as you can teach your child to chunk the word into smaller parts and then blend the chunks. For example, the word **cobweb** can be chunked into **cob** by covering **web** and **web** by covering **cob** and then blended to say **cobweb** when the whole word is revealed.

Phase Three Sounds

j	jelly	v	vet	w	wind	x	fox
y	yellow	z	zebra	zz	fizz	qu	queen
ch	chip	sh	ship	th	thumb	th	then
ng	king	ai	rain	ee	leek	igh	light
oa	goat	oo	moon	oo	book	ar	car
or	fork	ur	fur	ow	cow	oi	coin
ear	beard	air	chair	ure	cure	er	fern

There are a few more Tricky Words to learn to read in this phase. Help your child learn to read these words as sight words, sight words are words that are learnt as a whole and are not sounded out. The Phase Three Tricky Words are **he, she, we, me, be, was, you, they, all, are, my** and **her**.

Children are also taught High-Frequency Words, these are words that come up regularly in text; some of them are decodable, and some are not. Start teaching your child to read these words from Phase Three. A few of these words are also on the Tricky Words list. At the back of this book is a list of all the Tricky Words, High Frequency Words as well as Phase specific word lists that you can use to teach your child to read.

6
DEVELOPING SKILLS TO READ WORDS QUICKLY

Phase Four consolidates all the sounds taught so far. Children are also explicitly taught how to join two consonants alongside each other together. These are called consonant blends, and they can be difficult for children to hear. Words can have an initial consonant blend (**sweet**), final consonant blends (**hand**) or a combination of both (**stamp**).

When teaching blends, tell your child that they will join two sounds together, but will still say each sound. For children to become fluent readers, they need to recognise and read consonant blends. When children can read consonant blends, they can use them when sounding out unfamiliar words. For example, in the word **pump,** the final consonant blend **mp** can be chunked together, and the word sounded out as **p-u-mp**. Reading using consonant blends increases your child's chances of correctly hearing and reading a word. This phase is usually taught in the Reception year.

Phase Four Blends

st	stone	nd	hand	mp	lamp	nt	tent
nk	ink	ft	gift	sk	skunk	lt	belts
lp	help	lf	elf	lk	milk	pt	script
xt	text	tr	tree	dr	drink	gr	green
cr	crab	br	brown	fr	frog	bl	blue
fl	flag	gl	glue	pl	plug	cl	claw
sl	sleep	sp	spoon	st	stop	tw	twig
sm	smell	pr	printer	sc	scarf	sk	skunk
sn	snail	nch	lunch	scr	scream	shr	shrimp
thr	three	str	string				

The Phase Four Tricky Words are **said, have, like, so, do, some, come, were, there, little, one, when out** and **what.** At the back of the book there is a word list with all the Tricky Words and High Frequency words for Reception.

7
LEARNING TO READ UNFAMILIAR WORDS

In Phase Five children learn some new phonics vocabulary. A split digraph is when two letters together make one sound but are separated by a consonant; **a-e, e-e, u-e, o-e,** and **u-e** are the five split digraphs. Split digraphs used to be taught as "magic e" words. When you add a "magic e" on the end of the word it changes the short vowel sound in **pin** to a long vowel sound to make the word **pine**. When your child first starts learning to read split digraphs, they should presume that any word ending in an **e** is a split digraph and use the long vowel sound.

They also learn that some sounds can be made using different graphemes, and some spellings choices make different sounds, this is due to the origins of the word, these are called alternatives. Children learn to identify alternative graphemes (same sounds with different spellings) and alternative phonemes (same spellings for different sounds). For example, the **ai** sound in **rain** can also be represented with **eigh** for **eight, ey** for **grey, a-e** for **cake** or **ay** in the word **day,** these are alternative spellings (graphemes) for the same sound (phoneme). The spelling (grapheme) **y** can make different sounds (phonemes) such as in the words **pony, sky, yacht,** and **pyramid**. Children accept this idea easily and begin to ask questions such as "Which **ai** must I use?" These alternatives are often grouped into together as sound families.

Regularly remind your child of the alternative graphemes and phonemes; this will help them read unfamiliar words.

For vowel graphs your child should try the short vowel sound before the long sound as the short sound is more common. When your child encounters an unfamiliar word, they should try the first phoneme choice (the most common one) and if that does not work, they then try another sound. For example, if they encounter the word **spread** for the first time, they read the **ea** grapheme with the long sound and then try the short sound and decide which pronunciation sounds right. Teach them the saying, "If it (the sound) doesn't work, try, try another way." Show your child the different sounds they have learnt as often as possible so that they learn to recognise them quickly and accurately.

Phase Five Vowel Sound

ur	fur	**ai**	rain	**or**	storm	**air**	chair
ir	bird	**eigh**	weight	**our**	pour	**are**	mare
ear	pearl	**ey**	grey	**aur**	dinosaur	**ear**	pear
er	stern	**a-e**	snake	**aw**	saw	**ere**	where
or	worm	**ay**	play	**al**	walk	**aer**	aeroplane
our	journey	**ei**	reindeer	**au**	haunted		
		ea	great	**ough**	bought		
		e-e	fete	**ore**	sore		
		ae	sundae	**oor**	door		
		a	baby	**augh**	daughter		
ow	cow	ear	fear	ar	car	oi	coin
ou	house	eer	deer	al	calf	oy	toy
ough	drought	ere	sphere	a	bath	uo	buoy
		ier	pier				
u-e	cube	u	umbrella	er	letter	i	pin
u	uniform	o	won	ar	collar	y	pyramid
ew	dew	oo	flood	or	doctor	e	rocket
ue	argue	ou	enough	a	pizza	ui	guitar
oa	goat	oo	moon	ee	green	igh	light
oe	toe	ew	chew	y	pony	i	lion
o	no	u-e	cube	e-e	even	ie	pie
ow	throw	ue	blue	ey	key	i-e	pine
o-e	bone	ui	fruit	ea	bead	y	sky
ough	dough			ie	thief		
				e	me		
oo	book	e	bed	o	orange	ure	pure
u	bull	ea	bread	(w)a	wasp		
				ho	honest		

Phase Five Consonant Sound Families

c	cat	ch	chip	l	leg	t	tap
ck	sock	tch	watch	ll	hill	tt	mitt
k	king	t	picture			th	Thomas
ch	school					ed	jumped
qu	croquet						
cc	acclaim						
f	fish	j	jelly	m	mouse	n	nest
ff	waffle	g	giraffe	mb	lamb	kn	knight
ph	dolphin	gg	exaggerate	mn	Autumn	gn	gnome
gh	cough	dge	bridge	mm	hammer	nn	bunny
ft	often	gy	gym			pn	pneumonia
		di	soldier				
		ge	cage				
ng	king	r	rat	s	sun	sh	ship
n(k)	sink	rr	barrel	ss	kiss	ch	chef
ngue	tongue	wr	wrist	sc	scissors	ss	tissue
		rh	rhyme	ce	ice	ti	station
				ps	psyche	ci	suspicion
				st	listen	s	sugar
				ci	city	si	mansion
v	vet	w	wet	h	hat	b	bat
ve	give	wh	whistle	wh	whole	bb	rabbit
		u	queen				
d	dog	g	get	z	zebra	y	yacht
dd	middle	gg	egg	zz	buzz	i	opinion
ed	filled	gh	ghost	ze	amaze	j	hallelujah
		gu	guest	se	rose		
		gue	catalogue	s	bends		
				ss	scissors		
				x	xylophone		
p	panda	s	treasure				
pp	hippo	si	division				

Children also encounter homographs in Phase Five; these are words that are spelt the same but are pronounced differently. Encourage your child to read the sentence to understand the context of the word and then pronounce the word correctly.

In Year One the Phase Five Tricky Words are **oh, there, people, Mr, Mrs, looked, called, asked** and **could**.

At the back of the book is a combined word list for Year One. It comprises of Phase Five Tricky Words, Phase Five High-Frequency Words, the Year One Common Exception Words and the first 100 High-Frequency Words.

Graphemes with Alternative Phonemes

a	apple	what, bath, acorn
c	cat	ice
e	egg	he
g	goat	giraffe
i	ink	mind
ie	tie	thief
o	orange	no, mother
s	socks	sugar, cheese, treasure
t	tap	picture
u	umbrella	pull, unicorn
ue	blue	value
y	yellow	fly, berry, gym, python
oo	book	spoon
ar	car	warm
er	fern	teacher
or	order	work
ch	chip	school, chef
th	this	thin
wh	wheel	whole
ow	cow	snow
ear	beard	wear, learn
o-e	note	come
e-e	these	here, there
u-e	cute	rude
al	calf	call, capital
our	four	colour
se	house	please
ey	donkey	obey
ew	newt	grew
ea	peanut	head, great
ough	bought	plough, rough, dough, through
ui	biscuit	bruise
ou	cloud	soup, mould, could
ere	sphere	where
our	pour	odour

8
BECOMING A FLUENT READER

In Phase Six, children read words on sight without segmenting and blending out aloud. Most segmenting and blending will occur in your child's head with little need to sound out audibly. Your child will understand the mechanics of reading and should be developing greater fluency. As your child becomes a more competent reader.

Good readers have the skills needed to read any unfamiliar word they encounter by segmenting the word and then blending those sounds correctly to say the word. They recognise when a word does not sound right and use other sound choices until they have read the word correctly. They use sentence context to help them ascertain the meaning of an unfamiliar word and predict what the next word or sentence is in a paragraph. Good readers are not only automatic decoders of words, they use expression, vary their pace, change their tone, volume, and inflexion to capture the audience's attention.

It is vital to teach comprehension skills at this stage and encourage your child to think about the text, question what they have read, and make inferences. Your child has learnt to read, and now they read for learning. Children are introduced to homophones in Phase Six these are words that sound the same but are spelt differently.

Children start understanding morphology in Phase Six and read words with a variety of prefixes and suffixes. A morpheme is the smallest complete part of a word. A free morpheme is a whole word, usually called a root word, while a bound morpheme is a suffix or prefix. An understanding of morphemes helps children read unfamiliar words. In addition, an understanding of the meaning of the separate parts of a word, will help your child to understand new words. For example, knowing that the **dec**, when used as a prefix, means ten can help a child deduce the meaning of the words **decade** and **decagon**. Think of morphology like a tree. The root word is the root of the tree, and these root words can grow and change by adding prefixes or suffixes onto the words they then grow into new words.

Prefixes: come before the root word
re: rewrite

Suffixes: come after the root word
er: writer
ing: writing
s: writes

Root Word: is the main word
write

At the back of the book is a consolidated word list for Year Two; this comprises the Year Two Common Exception Words and the following 100 High-Frequency Words.

9
THE PHONICS SCREENING

The Phonics Screening Test is a statutory standardised government-issued attainment test that ascertains a child's ability to recognise, and blend sounds to read words to the desired level. The test is changed every year and covers the first five phases and takes place at the end of Year One.

The test is sent to the school and then kept securely locked away. Once the test has been administered your child's score will be confidential. The test starts with easy words and gets progressively harder. It is a combination of actual words and "alien" words. Alien words are made up words that are phonetically decodable. The inclusion of alien words tests whether children can phonetically decode and read unfamiliar words. Alien words have a picture of a little alien next to them, so the child knows they are nonsense words. Some children, particularly those on the autistic spectrum find alien words particularly difficult.

A familiar teacher administers the test on a one-to-one basis with each child and practice tests are held in the months running up to the screening; to monitor your child's progress and give them exposure to the process so that they do not experience anxiety. There is no time limit to the test, and the child's speech and accent are taken into consideration. Teachers are given online training before administering the test and are subject to moderation, so the process is as fair as possible.

All children are expected to sit the screening, but the teacher may stop the test if she feels the words are too hard for the child. Children with SEND are allowed to do the test. Coloured overlays can be used, and the font can be adjusted online to accommodate children with specific needs.

When preparing for the test, insist that your child sounds out and blend words that are presented in the phonics screening format, even if they think they know the word. Good readers sometimes presume they know the words and then get them wrong. They do not need to do this when reading normally, just for the screening practices and the screening itself.

Children love the experience and do not feel any pressure around the testing process. Parents are given the results after the pass mark is released, and the data is submitted to the Department for Education. Children who do not pass the screening will redo the screening in Year Two. The pass mark has been thirty-two out of forty for a few years now, but this is subject to change and is only made official after the screening.

10
READING DIFFICULTIES

If your child is falling behind and not learning to read at the same pace as other children, the first thing to do is to find out what they do know. Children should read for about twenty minutes every day to make adequate progress, if you are already doing this and your child is still not making sufficient progress then you might need to look at a few other factors. A child struggling to learn to read may battle with memory or processing difficulties, auditory or visual difficulties, poor fine motor control or a specific learning difficulty such as Dyslexia.

Memory or Processing Difficulties

Children struggling to learn to read may have trouble with memory or processing speed. Processing speed is the speed it takes to complete a task with reasonable accuracy. Some children may battle to concentrate and focus. These children will benefit from working in a quiet area.Some children may need some of the sounds re-taught before moving on to new sounds. When a child has blended a word, they should recognise the word and read it automatically. Explain to your child that they should say the word if they know it and do not have to sound it out. Children should only sound out and blend unfamiliar words. Some children take longer to recognise whole words, and they will need more repetition.

Auditory Difficulties

A child struggling to hear sounds in words may have a hearing problem and should have a hearing test. If your child has good hearing, they may have auditory perceptual difficulties and be struggling to understand or distinguish what they are hearing. Children with auditory processing difficulties appear not to listen, often look confused, take a long time to complete tasks, misunderstand instructions, or ask things repeatedly.

Auditory problems may comprise of one or more of the following challenges:
- Auditory Discrimination: This is the ability to distinguish between different sounds in the environment.
- Auditory Sequencing: This is the ability to recall words or sounds in order.
- Auditory Memory: This is the ability to recall what has been heard.
- Auditory Figure-ground Discrimination: This is the ability to focus on the essential sounds in a noisy environment.

Some children struggle with blending and as a result, they try to remember whole words. Go back to the pre-reading stage and start by segmenting and blending orally without letters to develop the child's auditory skills and then re-introduce letters. Play sound games with your child, say the sounds, and see if the child can blend the sounds to say the word. For example, say **sh-ee-p** and see if the child can hear and say the word **sheep**; do not give them any visual clues; this is a test to see if children can hear the sounds and blend them. Repeat the process in reverse with new words to see if a child can segment the word into its parts, say the word **ship**, and the child should say **sh-i-p**; this is a vital skill for spelling.

The child may have a short short-term auditory memory and struggles to retain the sounds heard or learnt. They will need to play lots of auditory games to develop listening skills and memory. Play word games like the "I went to the store and bought..." Help a child with a short auditory memory to blend longer words by teaching consonant blends; this reduces the number of sound chunks a child needs to remember and increases their chances of success. If your child appears to have auditory difficulties the first specialist to consult is an audiologist or and Occupational Therapist.

Visual Difficulties

Visual perception is the child's ability to make sense of what they see; a child may have perfect vision but still struggle with visual perception. Children who struggle with visual perception may look disorganised; they mislay things often and find it difficult to copy from the board. They may reverse numbers and letters and struggle to make their letters the correct size when writing. They find it hard to remember sight words and often lose their place when reading. They have difficulty recognising the graphemes taught and struggle to see those graphemes in words.

Visual Perceptual problems may comprise of one or more of the following challenges:
- Sensory Processing: This is the child's ability to interpret the messages he/she is receiving from their senses.
- Visual-Spatial Relationships: Understanding where things are in space and in relation to each other.
- Visual Attention: The ability to focus on important information visually.
- Visual Discrimination: This is the child's ability to see similarities and differences.
- Visual Sequential Memory: This is the child's ability to remember objects in order.
- Visual Figure-Ground: This is the child's ability to find something on a busy background.
- Visual Form Constancy: This is the child's understanding that a shape or letter remains the same despite its size or orientation.
- Visual Memory: This is the child's ability to remember an object visually.

Ensure that a child who struggles with visual perceptual difficulties has a clean, clutter-free desk. Keep their rooms as clutter-free as possible and put toys away in cupboards. Test your child's eye-tracking ability; the ability for the child to move their eyes along a line of text smoothly when reading. A simple check for this is to have your child hold their arm straight out in front of them, keep their head still and then move their arm in large figures of eight while watching their thumb. If the child moves their head to do this, or you notice their eyes bouncing, then they are struggling with tracking. There are simple exercises to help develop a child's eye muscles such as putting a toy car on the table and driving it from left to right, returning, and repeating the action, the child watches the car with his eyes while keeping his head still. Always allow children to use their fingers or a bookmark to follow along the line when reading as this develops good tracking skills. If your child is struggling with visual difficulties consult an optometrist, Occupational Therapists and Vision Therapists.

Poor Fine Motor Control

Some children may segment words correctly and yet are not making progress with their writing. Children with fine motor difficulties will struggle to hold a pencil and to colour or draw neatly. They avoid using scissors and tasks such as threading, using large tweezers or doing up buttons. They dislike construction toys and are slower to learn self-care tasks. They have poor posture and tend to tire quickly and lie down.

Poor fine motor skills may consist of one or more of the following difficulties:
- Crossing the Midline: This is the child's ability to cross the invisible line that runs from the top of the head down through the middle of the body through the nose.
- Finger and hand strength: The physical strength in the hands.
- Hand Dominance: The consistent use of one preferred hand for repetitive tasks.
- Bilateral Integration: The ability for the two hands to work together to perform a task, like holding a piece of paper with one hand and cutting with the other.
- Object Manipulation: The ability to use tools like scissors, a hairbrush, and pencils effectively.
- Postural Control: This is the child's ability to hold themselves upright through the trunk.
- Shoulder Stability: The shoulder strength and control needed to perform fine motor tasks.

These children need lots of activities to develop their fine motor control. Help your child establish hand dominance by watching to see which hand they favour and then encouraging them to use that hand for tasks. Demonstrate using two hands to complete activities, for example, holding a piece of paper with one hand while cutting with the other. Encourage play with activities that require fine motor control and strength, such as construction toys, threading, painting, and playdoh and provide lots of opportunities for craft and cutting tasks. The most popular fine motor activity I have ever had is small world animals wrapped in elastic bands, the children try to free the animals from the elastic bands. Consult an Occupational Therapist for a child who has fine motor difficulties.

Dyslexia

Dyslexia is a neurological learning difficulty. It consists of problems in auditory processing, phonological awareness, executive function, processing speed and working memory. Every person with Dyslexia presents slightly differently as they have different combinations of strengths and weaknesses. **However, the main difficulty with Dyslexia is reading.**

Children who struggle with Dyslexia may present with the following difficulties:

- Struggles with Phonics.
- Poor handwriting.
- Trouble remembering sight words.
- Lose their place when reading.
- Forget punctuation.
- Struggle to stay on task.
- Often lose things and are disorganised.
- Poor spelling.
- Leaves out, inserts, or guesses words when reading.
- Slow reading.
- Ignores or mixes up suffixes.
- Trouble with rhyming.
- Confuses the sequence of letters when writing or reading.

Children are usually only tested for Dyslexia from age seven but present with the symptoms from a young age. These children need multi-sensory learning experiences. Base all new learning on previous knowledge. The teaching of Phonics needs to be explicit and carefully planned. Use word families, mnemonics, and picture association to help children learn to spell. If by Year Two your child is still struggling to learn to read and spell, then it may be time to start considering learning difficulties such as Dyslexia. Children with Dyslexia may benefit from vision therapy, speech and language therapy, occupational therapy, and chiropractic care. Provide them with off white paper to work from to reduce visual stress, left align font and make the letters larger. Pre-teach and over-teach all language-based activities and allow plenty of time for activities, teach in a multi-sensory way.

Dysgraphia

Children need to learn to write with automaticity early on; this means that the child will not need to consciously think about producing every letter. Children should have developed this skill by Year Two to focus their mental energy on more complex language tasks. However, children with Dysgraphia struggle to learn to write letters, words, and sentences. These children may be labelled messy or lazy. It is a combination of difficulties involving fine motor control and visual processing. **The main difficulty with Dysgraphia is writing.**

Children with Dysgraphia show the following signs:
- Difficulty forming letters.
- An unusual pencil grip or handling of craft equipment.
- Tires when writing and complains of hand pain.
- Avoidance of fine-motor activities.
- Difficulty staying on the lines when writing.
- Difficulty spacing letters in words and words in sentences.
- Letter and number reversals.
- Slow, laborious writing pace.
- Oral communication is far better than written communication.
- Struggles with sentence structure.
- Poor punctuation.

Occupational therapy, vision therapy, speech and language therapy and chiropractic care can be effective in helping children with Dysgraphia. Practise writing using sensory writing activities and develop your child's keyboard skills to reduce the need for writing.

Dyspraxia

Dyspraxia is a medical condition that affects the movement of both fine and gross muscles. Children are diagnosed with Dyspraxia from the age of five onwards.

Children with Dyspraxia show the following signs:
- Difficulty with balance, coordination, and movement.
- Struggle to learn self-care tasks such as dressing and eating with cutlery.
- Trouble managing emotions and behaviour.
- Poor time management and planning.
- Handwriting difficulties.
- Immature speech and poor listening skills.
- The child looks clumsy.

Dyspraxia is diagnosed by a team of specialists, including psychiatrists, neurologists, physiotherapists, and paediatricians, as DCD (Developmental Coordination Disorder). Specialist treatment for Dyspraxia includes occupational therapy, chiropractic care and cognitive behavioural therapy; Pre-teach and over-teach physical skills. Provide lots of opportunities for children to play, swim, use play trails and engage in active play outside.

11
PRE-READING ACTIVITIES

Visual Perception

Visual perception is the child's ability to make sense of what they see; a child can have perfect vision but still struggle with visual perception. Most activities to develop visual perception occur in Nursery and Reception, but children struggling with these skills need to continue these activities.

Teaching Left to Right

If your child struggles to remember to read from left to right, place a green sticker on the left-hand side of the text or page to remind them where to start and a red sticker on the right of the page to show them where to stop. Use the mantra: "We read from left to right and top to bottom."

Puzzles

Puzzles can be challenging for children who struggle with visual perception. Start with simple puzzles and build up to more challenging puzzles with more pieces. Some children do not know how to build a puzzle and you will need to teach them how to make a puzzle.
1. Use the picture on the box as a reference.
2. Look for the corner pieces and put them in place.
3. Look for all the straight pieces and build the outside.
4. Look for pieces with the same colours, textures, and shapes to complete the puzzle.
5. If the puzzle piece will only go in when you force it, then it is the wring piece.

Bookmarks

To develop visual tracking skills children should use their finger or a bookmark to keep their place when reading. This helps train the eyes to move from left to right and focus on the word or sentence rather than bounce around the page.

Wooden Pattern Blocks

Wooden pattern blocks help children with a range of visual skills. These consist of 2D wooden shapes and picture instruction cards made from shapes. The child then uses the wooden blocks to copy the instruction cards. You can make your own or buy them in sets with activity cards for the child to copy. Children will find these tasks particularly challenging at first and will need your support.

Construction Games

Construction games such as Lego, Duplo, Knex, Magnetic Building Blocks, Meccano and wooden blocks help children develop spatial awareness. They also enhance fine motor skills and creativity.

Dot-to-Dots

Dot-to-dots are pictures created when the child connects the dots, these dots are normally numbered, and the child draws a line from the first number to the last number chronologically. Start the child on simple dot-to-dots and then build up to more complicated pictures. Pictures that look easy to an adult can be overwhelming to a child. Dot-to-dots develop fine motor control, visual figure-ground and visual spatial relations skills.

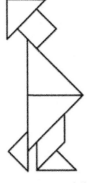

Tangrams

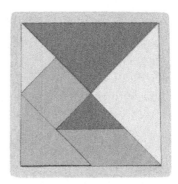

Tangrams are ancient Chinese geometrical puzzles that consist of a square cut into seven shapes. The shapes are rearranged to create pictures. The most accessible tangram puzzles show where each puzzle piece belongs in the picture, and the most challenging puzzles present the picture as a silhouette. Tangrams develop visual discrimination, spatial relations, figure-ground, sequential memory, and form constancy skills.

An Eye Spy Buddy

Make an Eye Spy Buddy by gluing a googly eye onto a lolly stick. The child then uses the stick to point at each word as they read. An Eye Spy Buddy helps the child develop visual tracking skills as well as fluency.

Coogam Wooden Shape Puzzles

Coogam makes a variety of different shape puzzles. The puzzles normally consist of shapes fitted into a wooden base board. The child then copies a picture instruction cards to complete

the puzzle. The activity cards range in complexity and suit any age. These puzzles develop fine motor control, visual closure, visual discrimination, visual figure ground and visual spatial relations skills.

Mosaic Block Pictures

A Mosaic block game is where square tiles are placed on a grid to reproduce a picture instruction card. Coogam makes a lovely wooden Mosaic Block Game that will last a long time. Children love copying patterns onto the mosaic board. They can make up patterns or designs or make words or shapes with the tiles. Mosaic Block Pictures develop fine motor, visual discrimination, visual figure-ground and visual spatial relations skills and problem solving.

Dobble

Dobble is a card game played with round cards; each card has several pictures of objects printed on them. The cards are shared out each player holds their cards face down and then takes turns placing cards face up on a stack in the centre of the table. If a child places a matching card on the pile, they quickly put their hand on the set and say the name of the matching item. The first one to place their hand down gets all the cards. The game is won when one child has the whole stack. Dobble develops visual discrimination, form constancy, figure-ground, and vocabulary skills.

Snap

Sets of snap cards are available everywhere. Share out the cards between two or three players. The players hold their cards face down and when it is their turn, they place a card face up on the stack on the table. When two consecutive cards are the same, the child says "Snap" while placing their hand on the stack. The first person to say "Snap" gets the stack. The game is won when one person has the whole pile. This game is good for visual discrimination and visual memory skills.

Complete the Picture

Give your child a picture with parts of the image missing. They then draw to complete the picture. If your child is new to this activity, then start with small areas of the picture missing and work up to pictures where half the image is removed. Symmetrical pictures are good for these types of activities. Complete the picture activities develop figure-ground, visual closure and spatial relations and problem-solving skills.

Q-bitz

Q-Bitz is a 3D puzzle game. The instruction card is placed on the table, and all the players replicate the card as fast as possible. The card can also be shown and then turned over, working on the child's memory skills. This game develops visual discrimination, form constancy, figure-ground discrimination, and visual closure skills.

Hidden Picture Activities

Give your child a page filled with lots of small images; children's mindfulness colouring books are an excellent place to find these. They then look for specific items and colour or circle them when they find them. Hidden picture activities develop visual discrimination, visual figure-ground and visual attention.

Hidden Picture Books

Hidden picture books like the *Where's Wally* books are great fun and develop visual discrimination, visual figure-ground and visual attention skills.

I Spy

Play I spy with the children. There are many variations of this game. Play with a game board, an I Spy Book or an I Spy Bottle filled with rice and small toys. When children are still learning to read and write, use the letter sound and not the letter name. I Spy develops a child's visual discrimination, form constancy, visual memory, and figure-ground skills.

Kim's Game

Kim's game is a visual memory game. Place a few objects on a tray. The child looks at the items and tries to memorise them. Then you cover the objects and have your child say what was on the table. Alternatively, cover the objects and remove one object and see if the child can identify what is missing when the things are uncovered. Start with three or four objects and build to more over time.

Pom-Pom Patterns

Create pom-pom pattern instruction cards by arranging coloured circles on a line. These cards can be made on the computer or simple stick circular stickers in a row on a strip of paper. Give the child the instruction card and they place the pom poms in order according to the card. This develops visual discrimination and visual sequential memory.

Heads and Tails Puzzles

Heads and tails puzzles are pictures where the children need to match half an animal or person with the other half. These puzzles can be bought, or you can make them by cutting images in half. These puzzles develop visual attention, visual discrimination, and visual spatial relations skills. Older children can write a list of the animals they make or write sentences about the animals.

Spot the Difference

Children compare pictures to find the differences. Start with simple images with obvious differences; this is a good activity for children with visual discrimination difficulties.

Egg Carton Patterns

Cheap plastic eggs are available everywhere at Easter time. Make simple egg pattern instruction cards using an array of coloured ovals. Your child then copies the instruction cards and puts plastic eggs into the egg cartons. Some children may struggle to do this activity due to colour blindness. This activity develops visual discrimination and visual spatial relations skills.

Blink

Blink is a card game that can be played with a small group of people. It is like Snap, except the pictures can be matched by the symbol, the number of objects or colour. This game is suitable for visual form constancy and visual discrimination skills.

Peg Boards

Peg boards are an invaluable tool for helping children with visual perceptual difficulties. Teach your child how to copy a pegboard pattern. Show them how to work from top to bottom and left to right. Pegboard patterns develop spatial relations and visual closure skills.

Mental Blox

Mental Blox is a puzzle game that can be played independently or in a small group. There are picture instruction cards; the child reproduces the images on the cards using the blocks. Mental Blox is excellent for visual discrimination spatial relations, visual closure, and form constancy.

Scramble Squares

Scramble squares are puzzles created with nine identically sized squares. On each side is the top or bottom of an animal or person with small differences. The squares are then arranged so that all the sides match up. They require children to pay careful attention to visual details in the pictures to solve the puzzle and give no self-correcting cues. Older children love these puzzles; however, children with visual difficulties will find these frustrating and need support. These puzzles are particularly good for developing visual attention, visual discrimination, and visual figure-ground skills.

Lollipop Pictures

Create shapes and pictures using coloured lollipop sticks and then photograph them to create instruction cards. Your child then copies the instruction cards using lollipop sticks. This develops visual spatial relations skills.

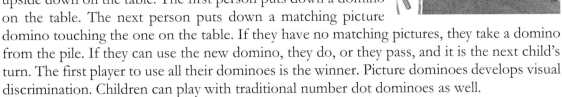

Picture Dominoes

Give each player five picture dominoes and place the rest upside down on the table. The first person puts down a domino on the table. The next person puts down a matching picture domino touching the one on the table. If they have no matching pictures, they take a domino from the pile. If they can use the new domino, they do, or they pass, and it is the next child's turn. The first player to use all their dominoes is the winner. Picture dominoes develops visual discrimination. Children can play with traditional number dot dominoes as well.

Lego Patterns

Create or photograph Lego pattern cards with brick towers of different coloured bricks and shape cards where the bricks create different shapes. Your child then copies the patterns using Lego. Place these cards and some bricks in a box to entertain your child while in the car. This activity can be tricky for children who are colour blind. This activity develops fine motor. visual sequency, visual spatial relations predicting and problem-solving skills.

Lite-Brite

Lite-Brite works on the same concept as a pegboard. Children copy pattern cards to create a picture using pegs on a board. When they are finished, they can turn on the light, and their work is brought to life using lights. The lights adds an element of reward to this game that children enjoy. Lite-Brite develops visual closure and spatial relations.

Geoboards

Geoboards are boards that have pegs or nails on with elastic bands stretched over the pegs to create the pictures. You can download geoboard instruction cards or create a pattern card by photographing elastic pictures on a geoboard. Your child copies the instruction card by stretching coloured elastic bands around pegs on a board. This activity can be tricky for children who are colour blind. This activity develops children's visual perceptual skills and fine motor skills at the same time.

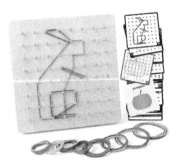

Rush Hour

Rush Hour is a traffic jam grid game where the child sets up their game in the same way as the instruction card by sliding their pieces on the grid. It comes with challenge cards on various levels and is an excellent game for a range of ages. It is a good activity for children with visual discrimination and spatial relation difficulties and children with processing and planning challenges.

Memory Game

Children love playing Memory Game. Place the cards face down on the table. The players take turns to uncover two cards; if the cards match, they can keep the cards and have another go; if they do not, they turn the cards back over, and it is the next person's turn. Memory Game develops visual discrimination, form constancy and visual memory skills.

Simon

The child watches a sequence of coloured light and then repeats the sequence. This activity can be tricky for children who are colour blind. This is a great game to develop visual sequential memory and discrimination

Numicon Pattern Boards

Numicon is normally used to teach maths concepts however they are also really good for visual perceptual skills. They come in sets with Numicon pieces, pegs, base boards and cards, the pattern cards fit onto the Numicon baseboards. The child then uses the Numicon pieces to make the picture. The picture cards can also be placed on the table for your child to copy. Alternatively, the child can copy a pattern created by you. This activity develops visual discrimination, visual figure-ground, and visual spatial relations skills.

Phonological Awareness

Phonological awareness is the understanding that words are made from sounds and sentences are made from words. All these activities develop an awareness of sound.

Nursery Rhymes

Sing Nursery Rhymes, songs, and chants with your child. Include lots of body percussion and actions. Songs with rhyme and alliteration develop an understanding of the similarities and differences in words. They develop speech patterns, intonation, cadence, and auditory memory and sequencing.

Mirror Mirror

Give your child a mirror, and they make noises while looking in the mirror or they pull faces and imitate the sounds and actions you make while looking in the mirror. Such as puffing out your cheeks and blowing bubbles like a fish, pulling a tongue, or chirping like a bird. This game develops auditory memory and auditory discrimination.

Vocal Noises

Use sound words and have your child copy you. These can be action words, animal noises or any other sound words. For example, you can moo like a cow or swing up high, whee or bounce the ball, boing, boing, boing or be quiet like a mouse, shshsh. This activity develops auditory memory and auditory discrimination.

Sound Ping Pong

Play sound call and repeat games. You make a sound, and your child echoes the sound back. For example you can say, "Ee-or, ee-or" and they copy you saying "Ee-or, ee-or." Or you could say, "Wheee-bump!" and they repeat, "Wheee-bump!" This game develops auditory memory and auditory discrimination.

Farm or Zoo Animal Small World

Provide farm or zoo animal small world toys for your child to use during free play. Encourage them to make animal noises as part of their play. This activity develops auditory discrimination.

Animal Masks

Give your child animal masks to use for role play. Ask them what noises the different animals make and encourage them to imitate the animals. This activity develops auditory discrimination.

Clap and Repeat

Clap a rhythm, and have your child copy the pattern. You can clap loudly, softly, fast, slow and vary the rhythm. This activity develops auditory memory and auditory sequencing.

Musical Statues

Put on some music and encourage your child to dance freely. When the music stops, they freeze, and when the music starts, they can dance again. This is a great rainy day activity. This game develops auditory attention and auditory figure ground discrimination.

Sound Stories

Read stories with lots of sounds where your child can join in with the sound effects like *Hairy McClary from Donaldson's Dairy* or What the Ladybird Heard by Julia Donaldson. This activity develops auditory memory and auditory discrimination.

Mystery Sounds

Record sounds around the house on your phone. Then play the sounds to your child and have them guess what the sounds are. This game develops auditory figure-ground discrimination and auditory discrimination.

Secret Sounds

Use opaque bottles, tins, or boxes, half fill them with different ingredients making sure each bottle has a pair. You can use popcorn kernels, beans, rice, sand, water, Lego, beads, or any other small object that would make a distinct sound when the bottle is shaken as fillers. Your child shakes each bottle and finds its' pair. This game develops auditory discrimination and auditory figure-ground discrimination.

Bottle Top Castanets

Glue two bottle tops on a piece of card, then fold the card over so that the tops can clap together to create a castanet. Your child then creates or copies musical beats using their castanets. Musical instruments develop auditory discrimination.

Rhythm Games

Clap out a beat and have your child move around the area in time with the rhythm. Children love to pretend so have them pretend to be characters while doing this activity, they could march like a soldier, hop like a bunny, or skip like a princess in time to the music. This game could also be played using a drum or a tambourine. These games develop auditory discrimination.

List Games

Start the game with a phrase and then fill in a noun. Your child repeats the phrase and your noun and adds a word of their own. Continue the game by each player repeating the list so far and adding a noun of their own. The nouns can be added in alphabetical order. This game develops auditory memory and auditory sequencing skills and is a great vocabulary builder.

I went to the beach, and I saw...

I went to the park, and I heard...

12
EARLY READING ACTIVITIES

Awareness of Words and Syllables

A child becomes aware of words when they start actively listening to and for words and playing with those words. They become aware of syllables when they can hear, clap or march to the rhythm or beat of words. Help your child hear and identify words in sentences with these games, hearing syllables becomes important when children start using more complex spelling rules.

Bedtime Stories

The most important thing you can do to help your child learn to read is to read to your child every day. Make reading part of your daily routine, pick interesting books with good vocabulary and good story lines.

March The Words

Say a sentence to your child, then repeat it while they march or clap to the beat of the sentence. Use one-syllable words for this activity as you are trying to demarcate words in a sentence. If you use two or three syllable words, it becomes harder for your child to hear the words as the syllables will insert extra beats into the sentence.

Count the Words

Say a sentence, then have your child repeat it while counting the words on their fingers. This activity is about saying the sentence and counting the words there is no writing at this point, you are trying to help your child identify individual words and understand the concept of a word.

Picture Cards

Print or draw a set of simple pictures and words. Show your child the picture while covering the word. They then say what the picture is, "tree." Then show them the word; this builds an association between words and their meanings. Your child is not reading the word; they are connecting the word with the image.

Bookshops and Libraries

Book rich environments such as book shops and libraries motivate children to read. They show them that books are valued by other members of the community. Children love libraries and many run regular readings and competitions, a regular trip to the library can quickly become a looked forward to family tradition.

Rhyming Words

Words that sound the same at the end are called rhyming words, they are also sometimes referred to as word families. Rhyming words are essential as children learn to listen for similarities and differences at the end of the words. Read rhyming books or play games where you and your child try to make lists of rhyming words.

Rhyming Tag

Say a word; then have your child say a rhyming word until neither of you can think of another word. Then again with another word. **"Cat, mat, rat, fat."**

Rhyming Basket

Fill a basket with pairs of objects or pictures of things that rhyme. Your child then finds and says the rhyming pairs.

Rhyming Books

Read rhyming picture books and point out the rhyming words or over emphasise the words and try to get your child to notice them. You could also have your child predict the rhyming pairs in the story; "I wonder what will rhyme with fox?" Julia Donaldson writes beautiful rhyming books but my favourites are Dr Seauss's books.

Rhyming I Spy

Play I Spy using rhyming words instead of sounds. Place some objects on a table and then have your child guess the words based on a rhyming word.
I Spy with my little eye something that rhymes with **dish**.
Child: **fish**!

Rhyming Alphabet

Say a word then show your child how to go through the alphabet to find as many different rhyming words as possible by changing the initial sound. Let's make words that rhyme with log: bog, cog, dog, fog, hog, jog and Zog.

Rhyming lists

Put a start word on the table and then set a timer and see who can think of the most rhyming words in a set time. Remember made up words are allowed as you are trying to teach your child how to listen for the rhyming section.

Initial Sounds

The initial sound is the first sound you can hear in word. They are the easiest sounds for most children to hear. When you are helping your child read a word say the initial sound louder than the other sounds as this will help them remember the sound.

Object Sound Game

Place small world items or pictures beginning with the sounds your child has learnt in a basket. The child picks an object out of the basket, says the object's name and the initial sound. This activity can be extended by placing the letter cards on the table and the children can match the item to the sound.

Sound Book

Create a sound scrapbook with your child. Write the grapheme on the page, and help your child find and stick in or write words containing the sound on the page. They decorate each page with drawings, photographs, or pictures of objects containing the sound.

Picture Sound Game

Print a set of pictures of things beginning with the sounds your child has learnt. Place all the pictures face up on the table. Have your child say what the image is and the initial sound. When your child is confident playing this game, you can place all the pictures face down and play again.

I Spy

Play I Spy using letter sounds. "I spy with my little eye something beginning with c..." "Car!"

Buried Treasure

Bury items that begin with the same initial sound in a sand tray. Your child digs up the things and says what they have found and the initial sound.

Tongue Twisters

Children love tongue twisters they reinforce initial sound recognition and have the added benefit of doubling up as speech therapy for children who struggle to say certain sounds.

She sells seashells on the seashore.

Betty Botter bought some butter.

I scream, you scream, we all scream for ice cream.

Thumbs up, thumbs down

Say a pair of words, and have your child show you a thumbs up if the words begin with the same initial sound or a thumbs down if they do not.

Parent: **bat/coat**   Child: (thumbs down) Parent: **bat/boat**   Child: (thumbs up)

Segmenting and Blending Phonemes

Children need to learn how to break words into their component sounds and then put them back together. These strategies will enable them to read unfamiliar words and spell difficult words on their own. Spend lots of time orally segmenting and blending words to build a firm foundation.

Robot Sounds

Call out a word and have your child say the sounds. Have your child pretend to be a robot while they are sounding out the words and move their arms in short jerking movements bending at the elbow with each sound, we call these robot arms. For example, you say the word **cat** and your child says: "**c-a-t** (while using robot arms for each sound), **cat.**"

Silly Simon Says...

Play Silly Simon with your child but sound out the last word. The child then blends the sounds, says the word, and does the action.
Parent: Silly Simon says stamp your **f-ee-t.**
Child: **Feet** (while stamping their feet).

Blending Cards

Print out a set of consonant letter cards on one colour card and vowel letter cards on another colour. Lay all the cards on the table upside down. Have your child pick up two cards, one in each colour, places them together, say the sounds then blends the two sounds. Play this game daily until the child is confident and blends easily. You can then add some new sounds or get your child to pick up two consonant cards and place them on either side of the vowel and ask the child to blend the CVC word. If they still cannot do this then, go back to blending VC pseudo words until they are ready and then try again.

Count the Sounds

Say a word, then have your child repeat the word, the second time they say the word they stretch out the word while counting the sounds on their fingers, then they say the word one last time.
Parent: **Ship**
Child: **Ship**, **sh-i-p**, -three sounds (while holding up three fingers), **ship**.

Sound buttons

Use small objects such as playdoh balls, cubes, or counters to represent phoneme buttons. The child uses one thing per sound and moves (or squashes if it is playdoh) the thing as they say the sound. For example, if the child sees the word rabbit, they should put one manipulative under each sound, they then read each sound and blend them together to say the word.

Phoneme Buttons

Create phoneme button picture cards. Each card has the same number of buttons as the sounds in the picture, this helps the child to self-correct should they have the incorrect number of sounds. There is no writing or letters, just the awareness of sounds. The child sounds out the word by pressing each button as she/he says the sound. If your child gets the snail picture card they say "**snail**," then they use their finger to touch each button as they say the sound in the word slowly "**s-n-ai-l**." To vary this activity the child could make four playdoh balls and place one on each phoneme button and then press into each ball as they sound out the words, some children may even enjoy smashing each ball with a fist as they sound out.

Phoneme Button Strips

Create phoneme button strips; these are the same as phoneme button cards except they are on strips of card. Remember children need to do the same activity several times for them to learn effectively, however if you present the activity in the same way each time, they will quickly get bored so varying the layout is one way we can recycle the activity. Each card has the same number of buttons as the sounds in the word to help the child recognise the number of sounds. The child presses each button on the strip as they sound out the word. If the child gets the moon strip they say "**moon**," then they use their finger to touch each button as they say the

sound in the word slowly "**m-oo-n**." To vary this activity the child can place a cube or counter on each sound button and move the counter as they say each sound.

Puppet Language

Puppets are a great way of getting a child's attention. Tell the children an elaborate back story for your puppet and give him an interesting name then tell them that the puppet sometimes gets confused and uses sounds instead of words, so they need to put the sounds back together to help you understand him. Then have the puppet sound out some words, and your child can say the words that the puppet is sounding out.

Puppet: I want some **l-u-n-ch**.

Child: **lunch**!

The Alphabet

Teach your child to say the alphabet rather than sing the alphabet song. When they sing the song **L, M, N, O, P** becomes one word and there is little separation between the letter names. This activity helps develop auditory memory.

Move It

Give your child some manipulatives such as counters, cubes, or balls. Then say a word, the child repeats the word then slowly sounds it out while moving one counter for each sound. They then count the counters and say how many sounds are in the word.

Parent: **Bed**

Child: **Bed, b-e-d** (while moving counters), -three sounds.

To develop phonological awareness, you can then ask questions or give instructions about the word.

Parent: Point to the middle sound.

Squash the last sound.

Move the first sound back and say the word without it.

Picture Cards

Place cards with pictures of objects containing the sounds your child has learnt on the table face-up. The child picks up a picture card, says the word for the image, then says the sounds in the word. At first, the child may only say the first or last sound, if this happens repeat the word and sound it out with all the sounds so that the child can hear them, with time and repetition they will begin to hear the middle sounds as well

Child: "Fish, f-sh, fish"

Parent: That's right, fish, f-i-sh, fish"

Sound Isolation

Say a word and have your child repeat the word, sound it out and say the word again. Then ask questions about the position of the sounds within the word.

Parent: **Pig**

Child: **Pig, p-i-g, pig**.

Parent: What is the first sound?

Child: **p**

Parent: What is the last sound?

Child: **g**

Parent: What is the middle sound?

Child: **i**

Consonant Blend Sound Counting

Say a blend such as **cl**. The child says the blend then segments it while counting the sounds on their fingers and lastly, they repeat the blend.

Parent: **cl**

Child: **cl, c-l** (while holding up two fingers), **cl**.

They can also tell you a word containing the consonant blend. Use both initial and final blends.

13
ACTIVITIES FOR READING

Reading is the blending together of sounds represented by letters to form a word. Children need to move while learning to read, and it should be taught in a multi-sensory way. They need to engage with what they are doing, have fun and move to embed the new knowledge and skills.

Reading with your Child
Read with your child for twenty minutes every day. Children who read for twenty minutes a day score 90% higher in standardised tests than their peers. Reading is a skill and like any skill it needs to be practiced regularly.

Reads **1 minute**/day
195 minutes /school year
21 hours by Year 6
8000 words /school year

Reads **5 minutes**/day
975 minutes/school year
113 hours by Year 6
282000 words /school year

Reads **20 minutes**/day
3900 minutes/ school year
455 hours by Year 6
1.8 million words/school year

Flashcards
Revise sound flashcards often using handheld cards or with interactive software like *PhonicsPlay* or *Jolly Phonics*. Your child should read the flashcards as quickly and accurately as possible as rapid recall aids blending.

Dots and Dashes
Once children understand the concept of finding the sounds in words using physical manipulatives, they can then move on to drawing dots and dashes under the sounds in words. The child draws a dot under a graph and a dash under a digraph, trigraph or quadgraph.

c l ow n
. . _ .

14
READING MATERIAL

Reading is important in all aspects of life and therefore it should not only be presented in books. Reading activities can be presented as letters, recipes, blogs, menus, notes, lists or road signs.

Phonics Reading Books

Decodable books or phonics books are books that the child can read independently once they have learnt the appropriate phonemes and graphemes. These books give your child practice and consolidate new knowledge.

They are normally arranged into levels and are often assigned colours to demarcate these levels. The child moves up the colour bands based on their individual reading ability. Match the book to the child's reading ability. An easy book will not challenge them while a difficult book will demotivate them. If a child can read roughly 80% of a book and decodes and blends the other 20% then you might want to try them on to the next level of reading books.

Printable Phonics Books

There are lots of printable phonics books available online and children like making and reading their own books. These can be used to consolidate a new sound, encourage reluctant readers or as an alternative to published reading material.

Picture Books

Reading starts with looking at books, then recognising letters and words and then reading sentences. Provide your child with plenty of picture books to enjoy. Exploring these books will help improve their self-confidence and reading motivation.

Chapter Books

Provide your child with chapter books early in their school careers. Good readers will discover they can read them, and this will boost their confidence. However, good word readers with visual tracking difficulties will struggle to read chapter books, have your child place a bookmark under each line as they are reading.

Reading Booklets

Reading Booklets are small, short phonics books. They can be re-used, given to a child as a reward or personalised by inserting the child's name.

Letters

There are lots of opportunities to read letters throughout the year. Your child could get a letter from Father Christmas, the Easter Bunny, Hogwarts School, or the Elf on the Shelf. They could even get a personalised letter from the Tooth Fairy when they lose a tooth.

Labels

Label everything in your home including the furniture. Put spelling words up on display and use words as part of role play areas, like menus for a restaurant or price lists in a shop. Labelling your home provides opportunities for incidental reading throughout the day.

Recipes

To vary reading opportunities have your child read a recipe to bake or cook something. These types of activities are fun, and inspirational, they motivate children to read on their own. Create a family recipe book of all the special things you make together, this will become a treasured family heirloom in time.

Lists

Provide your child with lists to read. When you go shopping, give your child their own shopping cart and list. They then find all the items on the list and put them in their cart, you could add a treat onto the end of the list as motivation to read the whole list.

Invitations

Birthday or wedding invitations are always exciting. Share invitations with your child and get them to help read them, put them on the fridge and refer to them regularly. Look at the elements of an invitation and discuss the expectations that are set such as the formality of the event, time, and importance of replying to the invitation.

Cards

Share Christmas, Easter, birthday, and thank you cards with your child. Encourage them to make and give cards for celebrations. Look at the format and elements of different types of cards.

Menus

Collect some takeaway menus from local restaurants for your child to read during role play. When you go out for dinner or to get take aways encourage your child to look at and read the menu and make their own choices.

Road Signs

Go on a walk to look at road and shop signs in the local area or print out some signs. These should be words and symbols. Symbol recognition is an essential part of learning to read. Most children can read the symbol for MacDonald's years before they start "reading."

Comics

Comics, or graphic novels, stimulate children's interest with their bright illustrations and action-packed storylines. Vary traditional books with comics in your daily reading time. They are also an excellent example of direct speech and use many different types of sentences. Comics can motivate reluctant readers and boys particularly enjoy superhero comics about their favourite characters.

Tablets or Computers

E-books or living texts are hugely popular with modern children who prefer them to dead texts (traditional paper books) as they are interactive. These books can be follow-along books (a narrator reads and the text lights up as it is read), read alone books (the child reads the book without help) or narrated/audible books (audio books without accompanying text). All these types of books have their uses, the trick is variety as the child can then develop the greatest range of skills.

Instruction Cards

Create instruction cards for your child to follow to complete tasks. You can also use ready-made instruction booklets like those that accompany Lego models. Remember that even though these booklets have few words, children must interpret the instructions from the beginning to the end, follow along step-by-step, concentrate, self-correction and problem solve. These are all essential reading skills. These

Word Cards

Create word cards for your child to read. These can be the Common Exception Words or based around a sound or phase. They can be used as flash cards, matched to pictures or the children can use them to practice segmenting and blending for the phonics screening. Play games such as memory game, Bingo, or snap with them.

Food Boxes or Cans

Look at the back of food cans and boxes for fun marketing stories. My cat food supplier has a fabulous letter on the back from a cat called Phoebe who tests the cat food before it gets sent to market, it is a real-world example of writing for an audience, persuasive language, technical jargon, and the structure of a letter. Children love things like this, and it makes them explore (and read) other packets and boxes in the pantry.

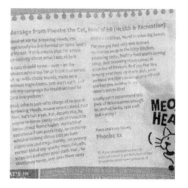

15
LETTER, SOUND RECOGNITION

Automatic letter recognition is essential for good reading. Children need to recognise the sounds for graphs, digraphs, trigraphs, quadgraphs and alternatives both in isolation and in words.

Phonics Pebbles

Collect some pebbles at the beach and write graphemes on them or buy Phonics Pebbles from Consortium. The benefit of the commercially available pebbles is that the children can touch and feel the graphemes that are etched into these pebbles. The pebbles can be sorted into sound groups, used to make words or you can say a sound, and your child can find the correct pebble. Play a game with the pebbles; place all the stones upside down on the table; the child then picks a pebble, turns it over and says the sound.

Surfing Sounds Beach Ball

Write some graphemes on a beach ball then play catch with your child. Every time each of you catch the ball, look at the sounds, say the sound and toss it to the other person.

Pouncing Game

Print a set of graphemes and lay them face-up on the table and then say a sound, your child then pounces on the sound as fast as possible. You can also print out the letters or words on A4 pieces of paper and cut them into the shape of puddles. Place them outside and say the word or letter and your child finds and stomps on the puddle. Give them an umbrella and a pair of wellies to make this activity more fun

Sound Detectives

Give your child a magnifying glass then tell them they are going to be detectives and they must find some missing sounds in a book. Tell them which sounds they are looking for or write them down.

Letter Auction

Letter auctions are a great revision exercise. Give your child a set of spelling choices on lolly sticks as auction paddles. Call out a sound, and have your child raise the correct paddle and repeat the sound back to you. Children love it if you use a silly auctioneer voice and style for this activity.

Alphabet Acorns

Alphabet Acorns are a commercially available game that reinforces letter recognition. Each plastic acorn is a tiny bottle and lid that contains a phonetic toy. Use the acorns for sorting, arrange them to form words, matching the letter to the toy, or have your child arrange them into alphabetical order.

Memory Game

Print a set of cards with the graphemes learnt so far and another set of cards with pictures beginning with the sounds learnt. Place all the cards upside down on the table. Each player takes turns to turn over two cards; if they get a pair, they can keep it. If they do not get a pair, they turn them back over.

Sound Snap

Create a set of letter cards, print each card twice to create a matching pair. Or create matching pairs by printing a picture and the grapheme for the initial sound of the picture. Share out the cards and play Snap using the cards.

I Went to The Zoo, and I Saw

Give your child an alphabet strip to help them play this game. Start the game by saying the rhyme: I went to the zoo, and I saw an, then fill in the name of an animal beginning with the letter **a** (use the sound and not the letter name). The next player says the rhyme, the animal that started with the letter **a** and thinks of their own animal beginning with the letter **b**.

Treasure Hunt

Print a set of graphemes and place them around the house. Your child then goes on a treasure hunt to find them. When they find them, they say the sound; if they get it correct, they can have a point for finding the grapheme and a bonus point for saying the sound correctly.

Sound Dash

Print graphemes in a large font on A4 or A 3 paper and place them in the garden or park. Call out a sound, and have your child run to the sound. For a bit of variation, call out a movement (skip, hop, crawl, slide) and the sound.

Letter Wands

Create magic letter wands by gluing plastic letters onto lollipop sticks. The children then walk around the classroom or playground, trying to find things that contain that sound.

16
READING MANIPULATIVES

Children learn when they move, physically engage with the task, and use their senses. Give your child letter manipulatives to make words; this keeps learning fun and engages their thinking skills.

Alphabet Beads
Beads with letters printed on them are ideal for making words. Beads come in different colours, sizes, and cases. Children find it easier to thread beads onto pipe cleaners than string. They can copy word cards, make up their own words or create rhyming words. When your child is first learning to read and write their own name, they can make a bangle or necklace with their name on to wear.

Letter Cookie Cutters
Give the children different types of dough, bread dough, biscuit dough, playdoh, salt dough or homemade playdough. They can roll it flat and cut out letters from the dough using alphabet cookie cutters. Alternatively, they can roll the dough into a sausage and use it to form letters.

Bread dough can be baked so that your child can eat their letters, this adds another layer of sensory input to the learning. Salt dough can be baked, painted, and sealed, and they can keep their letters and words. Add peppermint or vanilla essence to homemade playdough to enhance the sensory experience.

Alphabet Stickers
Children love stickers, give your child alphabet stickers to make words. Stickers come in different shapes, sizes, colour, fonts, and cases.

Wicki Sticks
Wicki sticks are thin strips of wax that children can manipulate to create 2D and 3D shapes. The child bends the sticks to create letters and words. Remember to give your child the words or letters you want them to make as it takes a huge amount of processing for a young child to try to imagine the shape of the letter, create the letter and then form a word.

Felt Letters

Make or but felt letters for your child to use on a felt board or a carpet. You can say a sound, and your child finds the correct letter. Or say a word, help your child sound it out and then make the word with the felt letters. They can also put the letters into alphabetical order or group them into consonants and vowels.

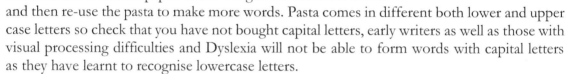

Alphabet Pasta

Alphabet pasta is a fun way for children to spell words. They can stick the words on paper with PVA glue or make the words and then re-use the pasta to make more words. Pasta comes in different both lower and upper case letters so check that you have not bought capital letters, early writers as well as those with visual processing difficulties and Dyslexia will not be able to form words with capital letters as they have learnt to recognise lowercase letters.

Blocks

A variety of blocks can be used to form letters and words, Lego, Duplo, link bricks, unifix cubes, wooden bricks, or Meccano. Teach your child how to make letters and then form words using the blocks. Put some Lego and word cards in a container to use as an activity when in the car or in a waiting room.

Alternatively, write the letters onto the blocks and your child then locks the blocks together to form the words. Give them a card with the word, as it is hard for children to think of words and then make them with blocks.

Keyboard

Use a real keyboard or one printed on a piece of paper. Give your child words cards with the words you would like them to practice, and they type the words onto the keyboard. Alternatively you can log on to a typing programme such as Word and let the children type their words and then print them. Children can also write the words in paint on a tablet.

Word Construction

Children love word construction tools; they screw the nuts onto bolts to create words. The different sides of the bolt have different letters on them, so they can turn the nuts to make new words. This also develops fine motor control.

Peg Boards

Peg boards are a good investment. They are excellent for a wide range of visual difficulties and can also be used to form letters and words. Give your child the word or letter to copy, the first few times you will have to show your child how to copy a pattern board. Children with visual processing difficulties and Dyslexia will struggle with this activity.

Matchsticks

You can buy bags of matchsticks from craft stores, your child using the sticks to form letters and words. Give them an instruction card with the words or letters printed on so that they have a reference when doing the activity.

Letter Tiles

Letter tiles are available from most good craft stores. They can be coasters with letters printed on, Scrabble tiles, Bananagrams or scrapbooking letter tiles. You can also print carboard letter from the computer. Give the child words to copy or say a word and you're your child sound it out and make it with the letters. Before using letter tiles check if they are lowercase or uppercase as early writers and children with visual processing skills or Dyslexia will struggle to make words with capital letters if they have been taught to recognise lowercase letters.

Wooden Letters

Wooden letters are available from craft stores. They are robust and will last for years. Your child creates words using the letters and then traces around them or writes the words. Wooden letters come in different sizes, fonts, cases, and colours.

Magnetic Letters

Children love magnetic letters especially when they are on the fridge and the whole family gets involved in making words and reading each other's messages. Magnetic letters come in different colours, sizes, fonts, and materials. Coogam have a set of foam magnetic letters come in blue for vowels and red for consonants, each letter has the capital and lowercase form and they stored in a box with the letters alphabetised into compartments. I love these and is the one resource I would recommend them over all others.

Newspaper Letters

Print a variety of letters from the computer or help your child cut out letters from newspapers or magazines. They then form words using the letters. Make the activity more engaging by telling your child the words are a secret code or a ransom note, and they are spies creating a secret list of words.

Dotting Objects

Give your child some gems, Skittles, jelly tots, dot stickers, buttons, M&M, Smarties or bingo stamps to place over letters or words. Please supervise small children with this task as small objects are a choking hazard.

Letter Threading

Letter Threading is different to alphabet beads as these are beads in the shape of the letters. The children thread letter beads onto a string to make words on a word cards.

Pipe Cleaners

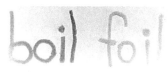

Give your child some pipe cleaners to bend into the shape of letters and words. These letters can be kept in a tub and used again on another occasion. Give your child word or letter cards to copy.

Pegs

Write letters onto wooden clothes pegs; your child then uses the pegs to form words. They can make up their own words or they can peg the pegs onto word or picture cards.

Wool

Give your child some wool and scissors to form letters and words. They can reuse the bits of wool or stick them onto paper. Write down words or letters for your child to copy. This task is frustrating for perfectionists as the wool moves and the letters will not be perfect.

Alphabet Shells

If you live near the beach, then collect some shells and write letters on the shells. If not, you can buy "shells" with letters already printed on them. Your child builds words using the shells. These are great for playing with at the beach or in the bath.

Natural Items

Natural items are cheap, readily available and provide children with sensory feedback. Pebbles, wood slices, sticks, acorns, and conkers are great natural items that can be used as reading manipulatives. Write letters onto them and have your child copy a word car or say a word and help them sound it out and build it with the manipulatives.

Alphabet Stamps

Stamps are an inexpensive and reusable resource that children love. Let them make up words, stamp their names or copy words. Stamps come in different sizes and fonts and you can also get different coloured stamp pads.

Bottle Top Graphemes

Collect milk bottle tops and write letters on them with a permanent marker. If you have two different coloured bottle tops, then write the vowels on one set and consonant on another. Your child then uses the bottle tops to make words. Give them word cards to copy or say a word and help your child sound it out and build the word.

Letter Dice

Letter dice are available from online retailers. They come with picture/ word cards. The dice have different letters on each side and the child uses the die to form the words on the instruction cards.

Spoon Letters

Use leftover spoons from take aways or buy a set of bamboo spoons then write letters on the spoons using a permanent marker. Your child can then serve up some words on a plate by placing the spoons next to each other to form words. Say words for your child to sound out and make or give them word cards to copy.

Mini Chalkboards

Mini Chalkboards are great for writing words. Say the word or give your child a word card. The child then sounds out the word and counts the sounds. They take out the required number of chalkboards, write one sound on each chalkboard and then place them in order.

17
READING TRICKY WORDS

Tricky words cannot be easily sounded out but are common in reading material, so children need to learn to read them by sight. Make these activities fun and involve the whole family.

Tricky Word Pebbles

Write Tricky Words on pebbles or buy ready-etched Tricky Word Pebbles. Hide them around the house or garden for your child to find. Play a game with the words by placing them upside down on the table and then take turns to turn over pebbles and read them. When you first play this game leave the stones face-up and let them choose which words to read out loud.

Tricky Words Memory Game

Print pairs of Tricky Words on cardboard. The children place all the Tricky Words upside down on the table and take turns to turn over two cards; if they get a pair, they can keep it. If they do not get a pair, they turn them back over and the next child has a turn.

Hidden Word Pictures

Write the letters for a word onto a picture. Then give your child a magnifying glass and let them look for the letters and make the words like a real detective!

Tricky Word Snack

Write the Tricky Words onto fruit snacks. Your child then reads the words when they have their snack. Only write on the outside of fruit where the peel is not eaten like bananas and oranges.

Tricky Word Sticks

Write the Tricky Words onto lollipop sticks and place them in a jar or tin. Your child can pick five sticks out of the tin and arrange them alphabetically. They pick a few sticks, read them, and then arrange them into a picture, like a house. You can play a game and time your child to see how many words they can read in a minute.

Tricky Word Bingo

Write Tricky Words onto a grid to create a Bingo board and then play Bingo as a family. Each player gets a Bingo board, the words are placed in a stack on the table. Each person takes turns to read the words in the stacks and the other players cover the words with a counter or Bingo stamper. The first person to cover their board is the winner.

Tricky Word Splat

Write the Tricky Words onto pictures of flies or bugs. Say a Tricky Word, and your child then splats the word with a fly swat. You can also play this game as a family with two or three people with a fly swat and a tricky word caller, the caller says the word and the swatters try to be the first to swat a word.

Tricky word Treasure Hunt

Write Tricky Words on strips of paper and hide them around the house. Then have a treasure hunt to see who can find the most or how fast they can find and read all the Tricky Words.

Tricky Word Beach Ball

Write Tricky Words on a beach ball. Then play catch with the ball, every time a player catches the ball, they choose a word and read it. This is a great game for a day at the beach or the park.

Tricky Word Target Practice

Write Tricky words onto the back of some wrapping paper or a large piece of card and stick it to the wall. When you say a Tricky Word, your child tries to hit the word with a soft ball. Alternatively, the child can throw the ball and say the word they hit.

Bean Bag Toss

Write some Tricky words onto a large sheet of paper and lie it on the floor. Give your child a bean bag and as you say a Tricky word, they try to hit the word with their bean bag. They can also throw the beanbag and then say the word it lands on.

Tricky Word High Five

Paint your child's hand and stamp their handprints onto card, then write the Tricky words onto the cards. Stick the cards up all over the house, whenever anyone in the family walks pat the posters, they high five them and read the word.

18
WORD READING

Word activities begin with VC and CV words, then CVC. Before moving on to CVCC and CCVC words, spend some time on initial and final consonant blends. If children struggle to blend, go back to oral blending, and then progress onto letter blending activities and then words.

Blends Match Bingo

Make or buy a Bingo Board with consonant blends. The caller picks a card, says the blend and the children with the blends cover their graphemes with a counter. Supervise this game closely as blends are difficult for children to read, say and hear, and the children may need support.

Talisman Card Games

Talisman Card Games are available from PhonicBooks. The cards come in sets that focus on a few sounds and are progressive. It is a simple card game that requires the players to read the words on the cards as part of the game. They have beautiful graphics, and older children will love them as the illustrations are modern and age appropriate.

Chunky Monkey Cards

Create a table with VC blends or write the blends onto a whiteboard. Your child reads each blend from left to right using the letter sounds. Repeat this activity regularly until the child reads the words quickly and easily. Once they have learnt the chunks, you can then start on CV chunks. The idea is for your child to recognise chunks of words quickly and accurately and decrease segmenting and blending. This strategy is also beneficial for children with Dyslexia.

sa	se	si	so	su
ta	te	ti	to	tu
pa	pe	pi	po	pu

Blending Dominoes

Make or buy blending domino cards. On one side of the domino is a picture and on the other is a blend. Each player then plays dominoes by matching the blends to the pictures.

Word Object Matching

Write a set of words that correspond to a group of objects. Your child picks a word, sounds it out, reads it and then selects the item.

Word Picture Matching

Write a set of words that correspond to a group of pictures. Your child picks a word, sounds it out, reads it and then chooses the image off the table.

Spelligator

Spelligator is a commercial game that can be played as a family. The game contains a word list so children can also play independently and self-check their answers.

Reading Blocks

Write sets of words onto Lego or Duplo blocks. Your child reads the words written on the blocks and then sorts them. The child can sort the blocks into rhyming words, initial sounds, final sounds, word families or vowel groups.

Buried Treasure

Write decodable words onto yellow card and then cut them out in circles. Take the words with you to the beach and bury them for your child to dig up buried treasure.

Minute to Win It

Place a set of decodable words on the table. Your child sounds out and blends as many words as possible in a minute using a sand timer. You can play this game regularly and keep a tally of their score to help develop intrinsic motivation.

Reading Block Spinners

Reading block spinners are a Montessori reading aid, they come with sets of picture and word cards. The child spins the blocks to make words and then matches the block spinner to the word card and the picture card. You can than ask the child to say or write a sentence with the word.

Robot Arms

The children pretend to be robots and they move their arms in jerky movements from the elbow. They then segment the word and with each sound they move their arms like a robot, once the word is segmented, they then blend it to say the word.

Race Car Reading

Make a picture of a road and laminate it so that you can write on it with a whiteboard marker. Write decodable words onto the racetrack, making sure there is a small space between each grapheme. Your child then drives their toy car slowly over the graphemes saying the sounds as they move from left to right in their "Practice Drive". They then get ready to race; when they race their car, they must drive over the sounds again but much quicker this time. The race officials are listening; they need to hear all the sounds and the word at the end, or the driver will be disqualified!

Child: **c-oa-t** (Slowly driving a car over the first time.)

Child: **c-oa-t**, **coat** (Quickly driving while sounding out the word again and then says the word.)

Word Cards

Print a set of decodable word cards and place them face up on the table. Your child picks a card, sounds it out and reads the word. Once they can read the words confidently, they play the game again with the words face-down so that they cannot see the word before they read it.

Train Track Blending

Tell your child they are going to learn to be train drivers. Write graphemes onto stickers and stick them onto a train track to form words leaving a space between each grapheme. The child drives their train slowly over the graphemes saying the sounds as they drive from left to right in their "Practice Drive." Then then drive their train over the graphemes again a little bit quicker until they can hear and say the word. Then they have passed their "Train Driver's Licence."

Trash or Treasure

Print a set of words; some of the words are real, and others are pseudowords. Place a bin and a crown on the table. The child reads the words, if the word is a real, they put it by the crown; if it is a nonsense word, they put it in the bin.

Picture Word Puzzles

Print a set of pictures with the name of the image printed underneath. Cut the pictures into puzzles by separating the graphemes. The child builds the puzzles to make the word. There are lots of commercially available word puzzles and some of these are self-correcting so children can work independently.

Word Books

Print or write a set of words with a common grapheme onto strips of paper. Make a cover for the book with the grapheme printed on the front and staple the words together. The child then reads through the words each day until they are confident with the grapheme, they can then move on to the next book. This activity is good for children with Dyslexia as there is only one grapheme to learn, one word on each page, lots of repetition and moving through the books gives them a sense of achievement. They can also think of sentences with the words, draw the words or write the words. Use the word lists at the back of the book to help you create your books.

Catch A Word

Children love ball games; I always use a beach ball as no-one can get hurt and nothing can get broken. Say a phonetically decodable word then throw the ball to your child, they say the initial sound and throw it back to you to say the next sound, keep throwing the ball back and forth until the word has been sounded out.

Parent: **brush**.
Child: **b**
Parent: **r**
Child: **u**
Parent: **sh, brush**

Word Puzzles

Give your child a word; they then cut it into the sounds and remake the word. This activity is beneficial when children are learning new digraphs and trigraphs. Give the child the word **sheep**; they cut it into **sh-ee-p** and remake the word. Print or write the digraphs in a different colour to make it easier for the child to see, then later, the colour cues can be removed.

Key Ring Book

Create key ring books of word families. The cards each contain an initial graph and a picture of the word, the word ending is on the last card. The child flips over each card to read another word, this activity reinforces rhyming words and is self-correcting because of the pictures.

Flip Flap Book

Make or download a flip-flap book. On the left of the flip-flap book is a set of initial graphemes stapled together. Your child flips open the initial sound, reads the word, and finds the corresponding picture card that is stapled onto the right-hand side of the book.

Word Wheel

Make word wheels from paper plates by writing initial graphemes on a small inner plate and word ending on a large outer plate. The child moves the centre plate to make and read words. They then make the word with magnetic letters, write it, or say a sentence with the word. *Jolly Phonics* has word wheels with initial blends.

Word Slider

Make, download, or buy word sliders. Your child moves a strip of card to change one letter to make new words. They can then make the word using magnetic letters, write it, or make a sentence with the word. *123 Homeschool4me* has some beautiful printable word sliders which are available for home use.

Count It

Cut out a strip of paper and divide it into a few blocks, this is called a phoneme strip and is used to sound out words, alternatively copy the phoneme strips at the back of the book. Say a word to your child, then help them sound it out and help them write one sound in each box. If your child has not started writing yet then place a counter, Lego, playdoh balls or magnetic letters to represent the sounds in each box.

House Building

This game is suitable for sorting alternate sounds. Write words with alternate graphemes onto lolly sticks and place them on the table. Cut out two (or more if you are doing more graphemes) triangles and write the graphemes on the triangles, these will form the roofs of the houses. The child picks a stick, reads the word, and then places it under the correct roof.

19
READING HARDER WORDS

Once children start reading, they encounter more complex words and will need strategies to read these words.

Digraph and Trigraph Words
When children are first starting to read words with digraphs or trigraphs in them they will struggle to see them as sets of letters. You can help by underlining the digraph in colour or writing the digraph in another colour when you write the word.

<u>th</u> r <u>ow</u> n

th r ow n

Race the Clock
Write a list of words your child then reads the words as fast as possible. Use the same words for a few days, and they can try to improve their time every day.

Bananagrams
Bananagrams is a great game for the whole family. Place all the tiles face-down on the table. Each player takes fifteen tiles and turns their tiles face-up and tries to arrange the tiles into intersecting word grids. The words must be read from top to bottom or left to right. They can rearrange their grid as often as they like. Whenever a player places their last letter face-up they call out Peel! Then every player takes another tile. The first person to use all their letters in a connected word grid wins when there are no letters left in the pile.

Boggle
Boggle can be played using the actual Boggle Box, or you can copy the Boggle board at the back of the book and write in letters. Each player writes down as many words as they can in a set amount of time. The words must be at least three letters long. They can go in any direction, but all the letters must be connected in a chain, and each letter is only used once in a word. Plurals count as separate words. Don't play this game with children who have visual perceptual difficulties or Dyslexia, as they will find it very distressing.

a	r	i	l
p	d	f	o
o	t	s	n
k	e	w	m

Compound Word Addition

Compound words are words made from joining two words together. The compound word butterfly is made from the words butter and fly. If your child likes maths then you can present compound words as addition equations.

$$\textbf{butter} + \textbf{fly} = \text{butterfly}$$
$$\textbf{butterfly} = \text{butter} + \text{fly}$$

Compound Word Surgery

Tell your child there was a terrible accident involving a pair of scissors and some words, and the words were all chopped up and you need a brave doctor to put the words back together. Then give your child the compound words which have been cut into the component words and a box of plasters, they then put the words back together using the plasters. To make this activity more fun give your child a set of doctor's dress up scrubs and a toy hospital kit. Remember the more children play and have fun the more they will learn.

Magic e Wand

Write a list of CVC words that can be changed into split digraph words with the addition of an **e**. Make a magic **e** wand with a plastic **e** stuck on a lollipop stick. Give your child the wand to place on the end of the words and magically change them. They can wear fairy wings or a wizards hat to make this activity even more fun.

Split Digraph Folds

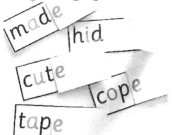

Write CVC words onto paint sample strips. Choose words that can be made into split digraph words with the addition of an **e**. Make a fold on the end of the strip and place an **e** on the outside of the fold. When the strip of card is folded over, it creates a split digraph word. Your child reads the word as a short vowel sound, then folds over the card and re-reads the word with a long vowel sound.

Split Digraph Ending In s

Children find it difficult to read split digraph plurals as the e is not on the end of the word. Write a list of words with split digraphs plurals, your child reads the word in the singular and then in the plural.

mates rates

makes capes

tapes cutes

Homographs Sentences

Homographs are words that are spelt the same but are pronounced differently. Write a sentence containing homographs and have them read the sentence and decide how to pronounce the word based on contextual clues.

> Wind up the hosepipe.
>
> He will read to his teacher.
>
> He shot the arrow with a bow.
>
> She read the scary book in the dark.
>
> The wind blew off his hat.
>
> Bow when you meet the king.

Paint Strip Contractions

Write the two component words onto a paint strip and then fold the paint strip to make the contraction by writing the contracted form onto the end of the strip. Have your child read the two words and then fold the strip of paper to read the contracted form.

Contraction Snowmen

Write the two words that are going to be contracted onto pictures of mittens. Then write the contracted form onto a snowman. Your child then matches the mittens to the snowman, they read the words separately and then read the contracted form.

Contraction Construction

Write the component words onto Lego pieces and the contraction onto a bigger piece of Lego. Give the Lego pieces to your child and have them build the puzzles. If you don't want to ruin their Lego buy cheaper building blocks or write the words on stickers.

Folded Contractions

The child folds a landscape piece of paper half and then in half again to create four columns. They then fold the two outside columns inwards so that they meet in the centre and look like wardrobe doors that can open and close. The child then writes the contracted form of the word on the inside of the wardrobe and the two component words on the outside of the wardrobe doors. If the paper is lined, you can write a list of contractions in this way.

Interactive Games

Interactive games are an invaluable tool that children love. They won't even realise they are learning and will beg to play. There are many great games available online; some are free, and others are paid, or subscription based. Phonics Play has both free and paid games. *Jolly Phonics* has an app that can be loaded onto a tablet.

20
CAPTION AND SENTENCE READING

Children learn to read short captions before they can read simple sentences. Not all the words in sentences and captions are decodable so it is important to teach children to read a few Tricky Words.

Caption Reading
Model reading a caption until your child starts to understand the concept. Sound out the first word and then blend it to read the word. Then sound out and blend the second word, then read the first and second word. Lastly, sound out and blend the third word and then read all three words in order. If there are any Tricky Words, point them out and read the word.
Parent: **b-i-g, big**
r-e-d, red. big red
b-u-s, bus, big red bus

Shared Reading
Read with your child by reading the parts of the text they cannot access and then stopping at the decodable words and encouraging them to sound out and read the word. Alternatively, your child can read a page or sentence, and then you read a page or sentence. Remember it is more important for your child to stay motivated and interested than to read every word.

Sentence Substitutions
Sentence substitutions are sentences where the nouns can be swopped out. There is a base sentence and then a set of noun cards, the child reads the sentence and then chooses a noun to change the sentence. This allows weak readers to practice the same sentence repeatedly to develop fluency and confidence. You child will particularly enjoy this activity if you use their name or a photograph of them as one of the noun cards.

Jessie went to the park.
She played cars with Mark.

Magnetic Words
Magnetic words are available from craft stores and online retailers. Your child can use the magnetic words to build sentences. They often also come with blank pieces so write your child's name on one of these so that they can incorporate their name into their sentences. Magnetic words are great on the fridge so that the whole family can play.

21
READING STRATEGIES

Reading animals are wonderful way to teach children reading strategies for unfamiliar words. Copy the bookmark alongside and laminate it for your child to use while reading. Explain each strategy to your child and point out when to use each strategy while they are reading.

Stretchy Snake: The child sounds out the word slowly, blends the sounds and says the word.

Chunky Monkey: They breaks the word into smaller parts or words then reads the word blending the parts.

Tryin Lion: They try reading the word another way using alternate phonemes.

Eagle Eye: The child looks at the pictures for clues.

Bouncing Bunny: They read the sentence skipping out the word, then come back and read the sentence filling in the missing word based on contextual clues.

Pointy Porcupine: They point to the words or sounds as they read.

Wise Owl: The child listens to hear if the word or sentence makes sense.

Stretchy Snake
Sound out the word, then say the sounds together quickly.

Chunky Monkey
Look for chunks and small words you know.

Tryin' Lion
Try it another way.

Eagle Eye
Look at the picture for a clue.

Bouncing Bunny
Bounce over the word. Read to the end of the sentence then bounce back.

Pointy Porcupine
Point to the word as you read.

Wise Owl
Does it make sense?

22
READING FLUENCY

Reading fluency is what the child's reading sounds like when they are reading aloud. Reading should sound natural, like speaking. Fluent readers read accurately, use expression, pay attention to punctuation, have a natural pace, and vary their speed according to the mood or action of the text. They read in phrases, show intonation by raising or lowering their voices and use stress when reading words in italics or when emphasising a word in a sentence.

Reading for Fluency

Struggling readers and readers with Dyslexia will find sentence fluency particularly challenging. Write some fluency cards for your child to read. Each card consists of one sentence, the sentence is slowly built up, on the first line is the first word, the second line is the first and second word, on the third line is the first, second and third word etc. until the sentence is complete. This method gives your child the repetition needed to develop fluency.

Hug
Hug the
Hug the rabbit
Hug the rabbit and
Hug the rabbit and the
Hug the rabbit and the cat.

Reading for Fluency with a Book

Explain to your child that you are going to practice fluency. Then demonstrate what fluency is by reading a sentence in a choppy robotic manner and then again in a fluent manner. Then pick an appropriate sentence in a book for your child to read. The text should not be too easy or hard. Cover the sentence except for the first word with either a finger or a bookmark. Your child then reads the first word; the bookmark is then moved so that the second word is visible. They then start the sentence from the beginning and read the first and second word. The bookmark is then moved to reveal the third word, and the child reads the sentence from the beginning, reading the first, second and third word in order, continue until the sentence is finished.

Punctuation

Show your child how to read punctuation. They should stop at a full stop, pause at a comma, show emotion at an exclamation mark and there should be a vocal inflexion at the end of a question. Encourage them to use the punctuation when reading aloud.

23

READING COMPREHENSION

Children need to learn how to read with good comprehension as up till now reading has mainly been about reading words and sentences but not necessarily understanding what they have read. Children with good comprehension skills talk about what they have read; they summarise, compare the text to other books or their own experiences, make predictions or inferences and express an opinion on the text. Copy the bookmark alongside for your child to remind them of how to think about what they are reading.

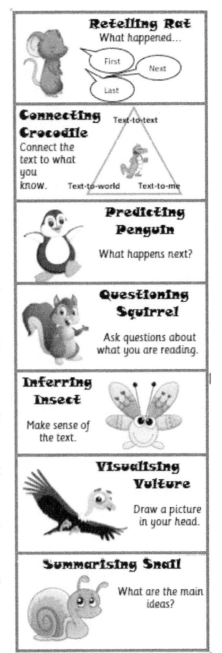

Retelling Rat: The child retells what they have read in chronological order.

Connecting Crocodile: They talk about how the text relates to another text, the world around them or their own experiences.

Predicting Penguin: The child makes predictions about what might happen next in the text based on what they have read.

Questioning Squirrel: They ask questions about what they have read.

Inferring Insect: The child makes deductions about what they have read.

Visualise Vulture: The child visualises what they have read in their head.

Summarising Snail: They summarise the main ideas in their own words.

Journal

Create a reading journal with your child. In the journal keep a record of the books they have read. The plays or movies you have seen based on books you have read. They can also record their thoughts and opinions about the books they have read. They can draw pictures of their favourite stories, summarise their favourite books or write book reviews. The more creative and interactive this can be the more your child will benefit from the activity. It will also make a wonderful keepsake for your child in later life

Discuss

Talk about books with your child. Discuss the characters and their motivations, think about alternate endings, and compare them to other books. The more your child can think and talk about books the better their comprehension will be.

Theatre and Drama

Give your child props and masks and encourage them act out stories. Take them to theatre productions of books they have read such as *Matilda* or *The Tiger who came to Tea*. Read the book first and then discuss the differences and similarities between the production and the book after the show.

Famous Authors

Take your child to famous author's homes or museums or to talks at the local library. Go onto author websites and read their biographies together or look for another book to read. These activities help children better understand different types of writing and the motivation behind books which leads to a deeper level of thinking about texts.

Questioning

Encourage your child to ask questions about what they are reading. Teach them question words, then ask them, "I wonder what question we could ask about the story beginning with who /what/ where/ when/ how/ why? Or email the authors with your child's question's very often the marketing managers will send an answer, your child will love this and it will encourage them to read more.

24
USEFUL RESOURCES

Letters and Sounds

The *Letters and Sounds: Principles and Practice of High-Quality Phonics* book lays out how to teach reading and spelling in a clear, easy to understand step-by-step format. However, it is not a government-endorsed book.

THRASS

THRASS is an acronym for Teaching Handwriting Reading and Spelling Skills and was developed by educational psychologist Alan Davies. It has a wealth of resources, stories, software, and tools. The training available with THRASS is far superior to any other phonics training I have completed. This system is hugely popular in Australia, South Africa, and Botswana but has not had the same level of popularity in the UK.

Jolly Phonics

Jolly Phonics is a multi-sensory, active (programme), specifically designed for young children (Lloyd, 2010). The computer software is easy to use, and children love the stories, songs, and games. The books are old fashioned and could do with a revamp, but the content is excellent, and they have a wide variety of resources. I would recommend *The Phonics Handbook* by Sue Lloyd and Phonics Teacher's Book. They also have an excellent online CPD course that is relatively inexpensive but highly informative.

Alphablocks

Alphablocks is brilliant. Children love these short little films in which "blocks" join to make words. Children start blending words quickly when exposed to Alphablocks as it clearly models blending. You can buy these in DVD sets that are progressive and develop their reading from single sounds to more complex digraphs, trigraphs and split digraphs. The books can be used in conjunction with the DVDs. If you use the books, then I suggest you watch an episode of Alphablocks to understand better how they want the child to read the book.

Phonics Play

Phonics Play is a subscription website. They have lovely flashcards and games that the children enjoy. The games are divided into phases

Twinkl

Twinkl has anything you could want for your classroom, activities, planning, intervention, displays and presentations. They are a subscription website but are well worth the cost; they are amazing!

The Oxford Reading Tree

The Oxford Reading Scheme is lovely. They have modern stories and pictures that appeal to young children. They are arranged progressively, so the books are never too hard or easy for the child and are now also available in electronic versions—no more worn old books, sticky from someone's spilt yoghurt. Electronic books are great because they last longer, are easy to access, and have a massive library of titles available and are good for the environment.

Bug Club Books

Bug club books are short phonics-based books that the children enjoy. They have the sounds and words printed on the back cover and some teaching ideas on the front cover.

PhonicBooks

PhonicBooks are written for beginner and catch-up readers. According to their website, they are arranged into a "highly-structured phonics sequence." The text is Dyslexia friendly and printed on cream pages. The illustrations are modern and colourful, High-Frequency words are "introduced slowly," and each book has a game to consolidate new knowledge and a vocabulary page. They also have a wealth of free resources for teachers on their website, including phonics information videos and reading diagnostic assessment tools. Talisman cards are also available through PhonicBooks.

Brain Gym

Brain Gym is a programme of short physical activities that develop the skills needed for the body to work and learn optimally. They recall the movements natural in the child's first few years of life. The teacher can use a book to do brain gym exercises, complete a course or become a facilitator. More information is available on the edu-k website.

Consortium

Consortium is a stationery supplier for schools. They have an excellent range of good quality, safe and affordable tools, toys, and stationery. In addition, they have lots of ready-made phonics games and resources that make planning more manageable and less time-consuming.

Amazon

Amazon has a wide range of educational toys and activities. They also have unique resources like Montessori equipment that cannot be found in local shops or stationery suppliers.

MyCuteGraphics

MyCuteGraphics is a website with gorgeous royalty-free child-friendly images in both colour and black and white. Use them to create worksheets, presentations or displays.

25
SOUND LISTS

Phase Two Sounds

s	socks	a	apple	t	tap	p	pot
i	ink	n	nose	m	mouse	d	dog
g	goat	o	orange	c	cat	k	king
ck	duck	e	egg	u	umbrella	r	rat
h	hat	b	bat	f	fish	ff	muffin
l	leaf	ll	jelly	ss	hiss		

Phase Three Sounds

j	jelly	v	vet	w	wind	x	fox
y	yellow	z	zebra	zz	fizz	qu	queen
ch	chip	sh	ship	th	thumb	th	then
ng	king	ai	rain	ee	leek	igh	light
oa	goat	oo	moon	oo	book	ar	car
or	fork	ur	fur	ow	cow	oi	coin
ear	beard	air	chair	ure	cure	er	fern

Phase Four Blends

st	stone	nd	hand	mp	lamp	nt	tent
nk	ink	ft	gift	sk	skunk	lt	belts
lp	help	lf	elf	lk	milk	pt	script
xt	text	tr	tree	dr	drink	gr	green
cr	crab	br	brown	fr	frog	bl	blue
fl	flag	gl	glue	pl	plug	cl	claw
sl	sleep	sp	spoon	st	stop	tw	twig
sm	smell	pr	printer	sc	scarf	sk	skunk
sn	snail	nch	lunch	scr	scream	shr	shrimp
thr	three	str	string				

Phase Five Vowel Sound Families   Short Vowel Sounds

a ant					
e egg	ea bread				
i ink	y pyramid	e rocket	ui guitar		
o octopus	(w)a wasp	ho honest			
u umbrella	o won				
oo book	u bull				

Long Vowel Sounds

ai rain	ay play	ey grey	a-e cake	ea great	a baby
ee bee	y pony ie genie	ey key (c)ei ceiling	ea bead	e me	e-e these
igh light	i-e pine	y sky	i lion	ie pie	
oa goat	oe toe	o no	ow snow	o-e bone	ou shoulder
u-e cube	u uniform	ew dew	ue argue		
oo moon	ew chew	u-e prune	ue blue	ui fruit	ou soup
oi coin	oy boy	uoy buoy			
ow cow	ou house	ough drought			
er ladder	ar collar	or doctor	a pizza		

Controlled R Vowels

air chair	are mare	ear pear	ere where	aer aeroplane	
ar car	al calf	a bath			
ir bird	ur fur	ear pearl	er stern	or worm	our journey
or fork	aw paw ore more	our pour augh caught	oor door ar war	al walk ough bought	au haunted
ear beard	eer deer	ere sphere	ier pier		ure cure

Phase Five Consonant Sound Families   Consonant Sounds

b bat	bb rabbit				
c cat	ck sock	k king	ch school	qu croquet	cc soccer
d dog	dd middle	ed filled			
f fish	ff waffle	ph dolphin	gh laugh		
g grapes	gg egg	gh ghost	gu guest	gue catalogue	
h hat	wh whole				
j jelly	g giraffe	dge bridge	ge cage	di soldier	gy gym
l leg	ll hill	le apple	el camel		
m mouse	mb lamb	mm hammer	mn autumn		
n nest	nn bunny	kn knight	gn gnome	pn pneumonia	
ng king	n(k) ink	ngue tongue			
p pig	pp hippo				
qu queen				x box	
r rainbow	rr barrel	wr wrist	rh rhyme		
s sun	ss kiss	c city	se horse	st listen	sc scissors
t tap	tt mitten	ed jumped			
v vet	ve give	f of			
w wig	wh whale	u queen			
y yo-yo	i opinion	j hallelujah			
z zebra	zz buzz	ze maze	se rose	s bends	ss scissors
ch chips	tch watch	t picture			
sh shell	ch chef	s sugar	ti station	si session	ci social
s treasure	si division		th tooth		th feather

26

WORD LISTS

Tricky Words
Phase Two

I	no	the	to	go	into

Phase Three

he	she	we	me	be	you
are	her	was	all	they	my

Phase Four

said	have	like	so	do	some
come	little	one	were	there	what
when	out				

Phase Five

oh	Mrs	people	their	called	Mr
looked	asked	could			

High Frequency Words
Phase Two

a	an	as	at	if
in	is	it	of	off
on	can	dad	had	back
and	get	big	him	his
not	got	up	mum	but
put	the	to	I	no
go	into			

Phase Three

will	that	this	then	them
with	see	for	now	down
look	too	he	she	we
me	be	was	you	they
all	are	my	her	

Phase Four

went	it's	from	children	just
help	said	have	like	so
do	some	come	were	there
little	one	when	out	what

Phase Five

don't	old	I'm	by	time
house	about	your	day	made
came	make	here	saw	very
oh	their	people	Mr	Mrs
looked	called	asked	could	

The Following One Hundred High Frequency Words

water	didn't	yes	through	lots	small
away	ran	play	way	need	car
good	know	take	been	that's	couldn't
want	bear	thought	stop	baby	three
over	can't	dog	must	fish	head
how	again	well	red	gave	king
did	cat	find	door	mouse	town
man	long	more	right	something	I've
going	things	I'll	sea	bed	around
where	new	round	these	may	every
would	after	tree	began	still	garden
or	wanted	magic	boy	found	fast
took	eat	shouted	animals	live	only
school	everyone	us	never	say	many
think	our	other	next	soon	laughed
home	two	food	first	night	
who	has	fox	work	narrator	

The Last 100 High Frequency Words

let's	clothes	different	friends	wind	white
much	tell	let	box	wish	coming
suddenly	key	girl	dark	eggs	he's
told	fun	which	grandad	once	river
another	place	inside	there's	please	liked
great	mother	run	looking	thing	giant
why	sat	any	end	stopped	looks
cried	boat	under	than	ever	use
keep	window	hat	best	miss	along
room	sleep	snow	better	most	plants
last	feet	air	hot	cold	dragon
jumped	morning	trees	sun	park	pulled
because	queen	bad	across	lived	we're
even	each	tea	gone	birds	fly
am	book	top	hard	duck	grow
before	its	eyes	floppy	horse	
gran	green	fell	really	rabbit	

Common Exception Words
Year One Words

the	a	do	to	today	me
of	said	says	are	were	she
was	is	his	has	I	we
you	your	they	be	he	no
go					

Year Two Words

door	floor	poor	because	find	kind
mind	behind	child	children	wild	climb
most	only	both	old	cold	gold
hold	told	every	great	break	steak
pretty	beautiful	after	fast	last	past
father	class	grass	pass	plant	path
bath	hour	move	prove	improve	sure
sugar	eye	could	should	would	who
whole	any	many	clothes	busy	people
water	again	half	money	Mr	Mrs
parents	Christmas	everybody	even		

Combined Words Lists

The following words lists have been organised by Year Group. The Reception Year list is comprised of the Phase Two, Three and Four Tricky Words and High Frequency Words. The Year One list is the Phase Five Tricky Words, the Year One Common Exception Words and the first 100 High Frequency Words. The Year Two List comprises of the Year Two Common Exception Words and the next 100 High Frequency Words.

Reception Combined Word List

a	all	an	and	are	as
at	back	be	big	but	can
children	come	dad	do	down	for
from	get	go	got	had	have
he	help	her	him	his	I
if	in	into	is	it	it's
just	like	little	look	me	mum
my	no	not	now	of	off
on	one	out	put	said	see
she	so	some	that	the	there
them	then	they	this	to	too
up	was	we	went	were	when
will	with	you			

Year One Combined Word List

about	again	after	animals	around	asked
away	baby	bed	bear	began	been
boy	by	called	cat	came	can't
car	could	couldn't	day	did	didn't
dog	door	don't	eat	every	everyone
fast	find	first	fish	food	found
fox	garden	gave	going	good	has
head	here	home	house	how	I'll
I'm	I've	king	looked	laughed	live
long	lots	made	make	many	man
may	magic	mouse	more	Mr	Mrs
must	narrator	need	new	never	next
night	oh	old	only	or	other
our	over	people	play	ran	right
round	say	says	saw	red	sea
shouted	small	something	soon	still	stop
take	today	took	that's	these	three
thought	through	their	things	think	time
town	tree	two	us	very	want
wanted	water	way	well	where	who
work	would	yes	your		

Year Two Combined Word List

across	am	air	along	another	any
bad	bath	beautiful	because	before	best
better	birds	boat	book	both	box
break	busy	child	Christmas	class	climb
clothes	cold	coming	cried	dark	different
dragon	duck	each	eggs	end	even
ever	every	everybody	eye	eyes	fast
father	feet	fell	find	floor	floppy
fly	friends	fun	girl	giant	gold
gone	gran	grandad	grass	great	green
grow	hard	half	hat	he's	hold
horse	hot	hour	improve	inside	it's
jumped	keep	key	kind	last	let
let's	lived	liked	looking	looks	many
mind	miss	money	morning	most	mother
move	much	old	once	only	parents
park	pass	past	path	place	plant
plants	please	poor	pretty	prove	pulled
queen	rabbit	really	river	room	run
sat	should	sleep	snow	steak	stopped
suddenly	sugar	sun	sure	tea	tell
under	use	than	there's	told	top
trees	water	we're	white	who	whole
why	wild	window	wind	wish	

27
WORD LISTS IN SOUND FAMILIES

Phase Two Word List

s a t	i	p	n	c	k
a	it	pat	ant	can	kid
at	sit	pip	an	cans	kin
sat		pit	nip	cap	kip
		sap	pan	caps	kit
		sip	pin	cat	tank
		sips	snap	cats	
		tap	snip	cod	
		taps	spin	cop	
		tip	tan	cops	
		tips	tin	cot	
		Unvoiced		If the following vowel is **a, o,** or **u.**	If the next vowel is an **i** or an **e**, use **k.**

ck	e	h	r	m	d
kick	neck	hack	crack	camp	and
pack	net	hat	crisp	him	dad
duck	peck	hats	ran	man	den
pick	pen	hectic	rap	map	did
sack	pest	hen	rat	mat	had
sick	pet	hens	rest	met	hid
snack	set	hint	rip	mill	mad
stack	step	hip	scrap	miss	red
stick	ten	hiss	trap	ram	sad
back	tent	hit	trip	stem	sand
At the end of a word or syllable after a short vowel sound.					

g	o	u	l	ll	f
gap	dog	cup	clap	bell	fan
gas	drop	mud	lap	doll	fat
get	got	mug	laptop	dull	fig
gran	not	mum	leg	fill	fin
grandad	on	run	let	hill	fit
grin	pond	sun	lid	mill	fog
grip	pot	sunset	lit	sell	frog
peg	rock	truck	lot	smell	from
rag	sock	tuck	plan	spell	fun
tag	stop	up	lost	tell	if
				One vowel and ends in an **l** sound, then use **ll**.	Unvoiced

ff	b	ss
bluff	back	boss
cliff	bad	dress
cuff	bag	fuss
fluff	bat	hiss
gruff	bed	kiss
huff	bet	less
muffin	big	mass
off	bus	mess
puff	but	moss
	rabbit	press
If the word has one vowel and ends in an **f** sound, then use **ff**.		If the word has one vowel and ends in an **s** sound, then use **ss**.

Phase Three Word List

j	v	w	x	y	z
jab	van	cobweb	box	yak	zap
jacket	vat	swim	exit	yam	zen
jam	vent	twig	fox	yap	zest
jet	vest	wag	mix	yard	zigzag
jig	vet	wax	next	yell	zip
job	vet	web	ox	yelp	zit
jog	vivid	wig	six	yes	
jump		will	tax	yet	
junk		win	taxi	yuck	
just		wind	wax		
At the start of a word.		Common spelling choice.	Usually at the end of a word.	At the start of a word.	At the start of a word

zz	qu	ch	sh	th	th
buzz	liquid	chap	cash	feather	cloth
fizz	quack	check	dish	slither	moth
jazz	queen	chicken	fish	that	thank
	quest	chill	hush	the	thick
	quick	children	rush	them	thin
	quill	chip	shed	then	think
	quilt	chop	shell	this	thirteen
	quit	much	ship		three
	quiz	rich	wish		tooth
	squid	such	shop		with
The word has one vowel, then use **zz**.	The queen **q** always has an umbrella **u**.	Usually at the start of a word.	Common spelling choice.	**th** followed by **e** usually makes the sound voiced.	Unvoiced

ng	ai	ee	igh	oa	oo
things	aim	three	fight	boat	boot
hang	bait	tree	high	coat	food
king	hail	feet	light	foam	moon
long	mail	jeep	midnight	goat	roof
ring	pain	keep	might	load	root
along	rain	see	night	loaf	spoon
sing	sail	need	right	moat	too
song	tail	sleep	sight	road	zoo
swing	train	queen	tight	soap	zoom
wing	wait	green	tonight	toad	
	When two vowels are together, say the long sound for the first vowel.	When two vowels are together, say the long sound for the first vowel.		One syllable words. When two vowels are together, say the long sound for the first vowel.	

or	ur	ow	oo	ar	er
born	burn	clown	book	bar	better
cord	burnt	cow	cook	bark	boxer
cork	burp	crown	foot	car	dinner
corn	curl	down	good	card	hammer
for	fur	frown	hood	cartoon	ladder
fork	hurt	how	hook	farm	letter
fort	hurt	now	look	hard	letter
sort	surf	owl	took	hard	rocker
torn	turn	sow	wood	park	summer
worn	turnip	town	wool	shark	supper
		At the end of a syllable.			

air	ure	oi	ear		
air	cure	boil	beard		
chair	manure	boil	clear		
fair	mature	coil	dear		
hair	pure	coin	ear		
lair	secure	join	fear		
pair	sure	oil	gear		
stair	lure	point	hear		
		soil	near		
		spoil	rear		
		tinfoil	year		
		When the **oi** sound is inside the word or syllable.			

Phase Four Word List
Initial Consonant Blends

bl	cl	fl	pl	sl	tw
blab	clam	flag	plan	slap	tweed
black	clamp	flap	plastic	sled	tweet
bland	clap	flash	plod	sleep	twig
bled	cling	flat	plop	slept	twin
bleed	clink	fleck	plot	slim	twist
blend	clip	fleet	plug	slip	twit
blog	clod	flesh	plum	slob	
bloom	clogs	flint	plump	slog	
blur	club	flip	plus	slot	

br	cr	dr	fr	gr	tr
brag	crab	drag	frantic	grab	track
bran	cram	drench	free	gran	train
brand	cramp	dress	fresh	green	tramp
brat	crash	drift	frill	grim	trap
brick	crept	drill	frisk	grin	tree
bring	crisp	drip	frog	grinch	treetop
brisk	croc	droop	from	grip	trend
broth	crop	drop	frost	grog	trim
brown	cross	drug	froth	growl	trip
brush	crust	drum	frown	grunt	trust

pr	sn	st	sc	sm	sw
pram	snack	stack	scam	smack	swam
preen	snag	stamp	scan	smart	swell
press	snail	stand	scar	smash	swift
prick	snap	star	scat	smell	swig
print	sniff	steel	scoff	smith	swim
promo	snip	steps	scoop	smock	swing
proof	snoop	stop	sculk	smog	swoon
prop	snort	stud	scull	smooth	swoop
props	snuck	stun	scalp	smug	swot

spr	str	shr	thr	scr	sp
sprain	strain	shrank	thrash	scrap	span
spring	strap	shred	three	screen	spark
sprint	string	shrill	thrift	script	spat
	strip	shrimp	thrill	scroll	sped
	stroll	shrink	throb	scrub	speech
	strop	shrub	thrush	scruff	spend
	strum	shrug	thrust	scruffy	spin
	strut			scrum	spit

Final Consonant Blends

lb	ld	lf	lm	lk	sp
bulb	cold	elf	film	bulk	crisp
	fold	golf		hulk	lisp
	held	shelf		milk	wisp
	sold	gulf		sculk	
	old	shelf		silk	
	bold	self		sulk	
	gold	himself			
		bookshelf			

lp	lt	ct	ft	nt	sk
gulp	belt	duct	drift	ant	desk
help	bolt	fact	gift	bent	disk
kelp	colt	impact	lift	burnt	husk
pulp	felt	infect	loft	dent	risk
welp	holt	inject	shift	hunt	tusk
yelp	melt	insect	soft	sent	
	quilt	pact	swift	joint	
	split	strict	theft	print	
	tilt	tact	tuft	tent	
				went	

pt	st	nch	mp	nd	nk
crept	best	bench	camp	band	bank
kept	boost	bunch	champ	bend	blink
script	chest	finch	chimpanzee	bond	bunk
slept	frost	French	damp	grand	drank
swept	gust	hunch	hump	hand	drunk
tempt	just	lunch	lamp	land	ink
wept	lost	munch	limp	mend	link
	must	pinch	plump	pond	sank
	nest	punch	ramp	sand	sink
	zest	winch	thump	wind	skunk

Phase Five Word List

ay	a	ey	a-e	eigh	ea
Friday	acorn	disobey	base	eight	great
may	angel	grey	cake	eighteen	break
Monday	apricot	obey	came	eighty	steak
play	apron	prey	take	freight	
pray	baby	survey	lake	neighbour	
Saturday	bacon	they	made	neighbourhood	
say	bagel		make	sleigh	
Sunday	basic		place	weight	
way	lady		shake		
away	nation		gave		
day	native				
At the end of a word			The **e** on the end of a split digraph makes the vowel say its name.		

ere	ear	are	a	al
everywhere	bear	bare	branch	balm
nowhere	pear	care	fast	calf
somewhere	swear	dare	faster	calm
there	tear	fare	father	half
where	wear	glare	grass	palm
		hare	last	
		scare	mast	
		share	pass	
		square	password	
		stare	past	
			path	
			ar in the south of England.	

ey	ea	ie	y	e	e-e
chimney	bead	belief	baby	be	complete
donkey	bean	chief	ferry	decent	even
honey	eat	field	funny	frequent	extreme
jockey	each	genie	every	he	gene
key	meat	priest	happy	me	scene
money	please	relief	floppy	recent	theme
monkey	read	shield	penny	she	these
trolley	tea	shriek	silly	we	
turkey	sea	thief	really	began	
valley	steam	yield	very	we're	

When two vowels are together, say the long sound for the first vowel.

At the end of a two-syllable word.

The **e** on the end of a split digraph makes the vowel say its name.

ea	ere	eer	o	a	oy
bread	adhere	beer	something	gorilla	annoy
breakfast	here	career	come	panda	annoying
dead	interfere	cheer	done	pizza	boy
deadly	severe	deer	Monday	banana	destroy
feather	sphere	peer	month	alone	enjoy
head		sheer	mother	ago	joy
heaven		steer	nothing	comma	oyster
instead		veer	other	idea	royal
read			some		toy
ready			another		

Schwa sound. Normally at the end of a word.

At the end of a word or syllable.

er	or	ear	ir	ou	ough
fern	word	early	bird	about	drought
her	work	earn	birth	around	plough
herbal	world	earnest	first	found	
herbs	worm	earth	girl	house	
jerky	worse	heard	shirt	loudest	
perky	worship	learn	sir	mouse	
permanent	worst	pearl	skirt	our	
servant	worth	rehearsal	thirsty	out	
stern	worthy	search	thirteen	shout	
verb			thirty	round	

Beginning or middle of a syllable.

y	ui		ie	i-e	i	y
bicycle	biscuit		cried	inside	behind	by
crystal	build		denied	invite	blind	cry
cygnet	guitar		die	kite	child	dry
Egypt			dried	wife	find	fly
gym			fried	like	giant	fry
mystery			lie	pine	kind	my
pyramid			pie	ripe	mild	reply
pyjamas			spied	shine	mind	sky
			tie	white	remind	spy
			tried	time	wild	why
			At the end of a word. Or to replace the **y** when the suffix **ed** is added to a root word.	The **e** on the end of a split digraph makes the vowel say its name.		When a short word ends with an **igh** sound.

a	(qu)a		u-e	u	ew	ue
swamp	qualify		computer	duty	dew	argue
swan	quantity		cube	future	few	cue
wallet	quarry		cute	human	knew	due
was	squabble		fuse	music	nephew	hue
wash	squadron		huge	stupid	new	rescue
wasp	squalid		mule	tuba	news	statue
watch	squander		muse	unicorn	newt	sue
what	squash		refuge	union	renew	value
swallow	squat		tube	unit	stew	venue
what	squad		use			
After a **w** or a **qu** an **a** makes an **o** sound			The **e** on the end of a split digraph makes the vowel say its name.			

o-e	o	ou	oe	ow	ou gh
alone	cold	boulder	doe	arrow	dough
bone	don't	mould	dominoes	grow	dough
envelope	go	mouldy	foe	low	nut
explode	gold	shoulder	goes	shadow	though
home	going		heroes	show	
note	told		hoe	slow	
pole	most		potatoes	snow	
stone	no		toe	know	
those	old		tomatoes	swallow	
woke	only		woe	window	
The **e** on the end of a split digraph makes the vowel say its name.		When two vowels are together, we say the long sound for the first vowel.			

ue	ew	u-e	ou	ui	o
blue	blew	brute	group	bruise	do
clue	chew	exclude	soup	cruise	to
cue	crew	flute	troupe	fluid	who
duel	drew	June	you	fruit	into
fuel	flew	plume	through	juice	
glue	grew	prune		nuisance	
issue	grew	rude		ruin	
tissue	screw	rule		suit	
true	threw	salute			
At the end of a word. When two vowels are together, say the long sound for the first vowel.	At the end of a word				

aw	au	our	oor	augh	ore
claw	August	court	door	caught	before
crawl	author	four	doorstep	daughter	chore
draw	automatic	fourth	doorstop	haughty	core
jaw	fraud	mourn	floor	naughty	more
law	haul	pour	poor	taught	score
lawn	haunted	tour	poorly		shore
paw	jaunty	tournament			snore
raw	launch	your			sore
saw	sauce				store
yawn	staunch				wore
In the middle or at the end of a word.	Never at the end of a word.				At the end of a word.

al	ar	ough	ch	tch	t
ball	towards	bought	chemical	catch	adventure
beanstalk	war	fought	chemist	ditch	capture
call	warm	ought	chord	fetch	creature
fall		thought	chorus	kitchen	feature
hall			Christmas	match	future
stalk			chronic	patch	mixture
talk			headache	pitch	nature
walk			school	scratch	picture
wall			technical	stitches	puncture
				witch	signature
	After a **w**.			After a single vowel letter.	When the **ch** sound is before **ure** or **ion**.

ph	wh	dge	g	le	el
alphabet	who	badge	danger	apple	camel
dolphin	whoever	badger	energy	bottle	squirrel
elephant	whole	dodge	gem	cattle	tinsel
graph	whom	fudge	gentle	giggle	towel
nephew	whose	hedge	giant	jumble	travel
phantom		ledge	ginger	little	tunnel
phonics		lodge	giraffe	middle	
prophet		lodger	gymnastics	table	
sphinx		sledge	magic	title	
telephone		wedge	magician	wiggle	
		After a short vowel sound at the end of a word	A **g** followed by the letter **e, i** or **y**.	At the end of a word, Adds a syllable to the word.	After **m, n, r, s, w, v, s**

mb	gn	kn	wr	wh	ve
bomb	assign	knee	winkle	what	above
climb	design	knew	wrap	wheel	behave
comb	gnat	knickers	wreck	when	brave
crumb	gnaw	knife	wren	where	gave
dumb	gnaw	knight	wrestle	which	give
lamb	gnome	knit	write	while	have
limb	gnu	knob	written	whisper	live
numb	resign	knock	wrong	whistle	love
plumbing	sign	know	wrote	white	save
thumb		knuckle	wry	why	wave
At the end of a word	At the beginning of a word.		At the beginning of a word.	At the start of a word.	An e must follow a v sound at the end of a word.

ch	ci	ti	s
brochure	ancient	caption	compression
chalet	artificial	mention	decision
chef	facial	motion	discussion
machine	financial	nutritious	fusion
	glacial	partial	mission
	musician	patience	passion
	official	position	session
	precious	potential	sugar
	social	potion	sure
	special	station	vision
Words with a French origin.	Words that end with **cial, cian,** or **cious.**	Words that end in **tion, tious,** or **tial.**	Words that end with **sion** or **ssion.**

se	sc	c	st	s	se
cease	crescent	acid	bristle	casual	because
crease	descent	advice	castle	leisure	browse
grease	fascinate	bicycle	Christmas	pleasure	cheese
grouse	fascinating	cell	glisten	television	ease
horse	scene	cellar	jostle	treasure	noise
house	scenery	central	listen	usual	pause
loose	scent	city	rustle	vision	please
mouse	science	ice	soften	visit	tease
purse	scissors	ice-cream	whistle		
		icicle	wrestle		
		A c followed by **e, i** or **y** makes an **s** sound.	Usually, in the middle of a word.		The **z** sound at the end of a word.

Phase Six Word List

ed	ing	ing	en	ness	less
cried	caring	giving	broaden	coldness	careless
jumped	carrying	having	flatten	darkness	clueless
landed	dancing	living	lengthen	fondness	helpless
liked	eating	loving	loosen	happiness	homeless
listened	feeling	saving	moisten	homelessness	hopeless
looked	flying		shorten	loneliness	painless
shredded	getting		soften	sadness	penniless
smiled	hoping		straighten	sickness	powerless
stopped	hopping		tighten	stillness	restless
wanted	meeting		toughen	tiredness	useless
Change a verb to past tense by adding **ed** if it ends in a consonant after a short vowel, double the consonant.	Present continuous. When you add **ing** to words that end in **ve**, drop the e.		The suffix **en** turns adjectives into verbs.	The suffix **ness** turns an adjective into a noun	The suffix **less** turns a noun or verb into an adjective.

er	er	ier	est	ment	ful
carer	bigger	angrier	biggest	advertisement	beautiful
listener	fatter	bumpier	coldest	agreement	careful
player	longer	crazier	fastest	amazement	hopeful
reader	nicer	dirtier	funniest	amusement	mouthful
rider	richer	earlier	hottest	development	painful
ruler	taller	foggier	longest	disagreement	playful
runner	thinner	funnier	nicest	employment	powerful
teacher	whiter	hairier	smallest	enjoyment	restful
worker	colder	happier	tallest	entertainment	thoughtful
	hotter	messier	whitest	payment	wonderful
	wetter				restful
Suffix **er** is added to a root word to make it the person who does the task.	A comparative adjective is used to compare two objects, animals, people, or ideas.		Superlatives are used to compare two or more objects, people, animals, or things.	Turn a verb into a noun.	Turn a noun or verb into an adjective, meaning full of/lots of something.

ly	ly	ly	un	y
badly	annually	brotherly	unafraid	bony
carefully	daily	friendly	unclear	cheeky
heavily	fortnightly	homely	undo	funny
kindly	hourly	motherly	unemployed	hairy
loudly	monthly	sisterly	unfair	noisy
quickly	weekly	fatherly	unhappy	nosy
quietly	yearly		unhealthy	smelly
safely			unkind	sunny
slowly			unload	muddy
suddenly			unlock	berry
Add **ly** to an adjective to change it to an adverb.	Add **ly** to a noun to change it to a time adverbial.	Add **ly** onto nouns to change them to adjectives.	The prefix **un** means the opposite.	It is used to change a noun to an adjective.

il	s/es	s/es	ies	
fossil	cries	birds	babies	ate
evil	drinks	books	berries	caught
lentil	eats	brushes	ladies	had
gerbil	feels	clothes	puppies	had
nostril	gets	boxes	leaves	ran
stencil	goes	hairs	knives	said
brazil	has	dishes	roofs	swam
until	sees	riches	shelves	thought
pupil	thinks	pushes	wolves	was
tonsil	plants	dresses	wives	swam
	The verb changed from the first person to the third person—the **y** changes to **ies.**	If it ends in **s, ss, x, ch,** or **sh,** add **es.** When the plural creates another syllable, then add **es.**	Plural. When the singular ends in **y,** drop the **y** and add **ies.** It ends in an **f** change to **v** and add **es.**	Irregular past tense verbs.

ei	ei	Contractions	Possessives
ceiling	abseil	he'd	child's
conceive	beige	I've	boy's
deceive	reign	she'll	boys'
receipt	reindeer	they'd	children's
receive	veil	they've	her
deceit	vein	we'll	his
perceive		don't	theirs'
		aren't	girl's
		she's	girls'
		I'm	
Place the **i** before **e** except after **c** when the sound is long.		If the subject is singular, place the apostrophe before the **s**; if it is plural, put the apostrophe after the s.	

Homophones

their/there	role/roll	soar/sore	weak/week
pair/pear	blew/blue	toe/tow	meet/meat
eight/ate	tail/tale	to/too/two	flour/flower
right/write	see/sea	tide/tied	for/four
vein/vain	sun/son	waste/waist	grate/great
I/eye	band/banned	bear/bare	fir/fur
new/knew	sew/so	some/sum	wood/would
by/buy/bye	band/banned	rows/rose	maid/made
been/bean	beach/beech	owe/oh	hour/our
whole/hole	be/bee	sum/some	bare/bear
root/route	way/weigh	so/sow	role/roll
scent/sent	wring/ring	not/knot	deer/dear
hour/our	write/right	night/knight	die/dye
won/one	tow/toe	tea/tee	hair/hare
heel/heal	know/no	red/read	mail/male

Contractions

will	are	is	not	have	had
he'll	they're	he's	can't	I've	he'd
I'll	what're	she's	aren't	they've	I'd
she'll	who're	it's	hasn't	we've	she'd
they'll	you're	that's	hadn't	who've	they'd
we'll		there's	wouldn't	you've	we'd
who'll		what's	won't		who'd
you'll		where's	mustn't		you'd

28
CAPTIONS AND SENTENCES

Phase Two Caption and Sentences

Mum is sad.

Cat and dog can dig.

I can see a rat.

A cat can nap.

A pig in a bin.

A fat cat.

A big red bus.

A pin on a map.

It is Sam.

Run to Dad.

Mum is sick.

It is Dad.

It is fun.

Pick up the mug and the cup.

Fill the bucket.

Hug the rabbit and the cat.

Go to bed.

The bug is fat.

Phase Three Sentences

Mark had fish and chips on a dish.

Dad has tools in a shed.

I see sixteen trees.

The ship hits the rocks with a thud.

Lots of shops sell chicken.

I am in a rush to get fish and chips.

A man is rich if he has lots of cash.

This weekend I will go camping.

Jim has six silver coins.

I can hear an owl hoot at night.

Nan sits in a rocking chair.

Bow down to the king and queen.

I can hear an owl hoot at night.

Bow down to the king and queen.

It has been hot this year.

Jill has six silver coins.

I can see a pair of boots on the mat.

I got wet in the rain.

Nan sits in the rocking chair.

I can see a pair of boots on the mat.

Stan had a chat with his dad.

Phase Four Sentences

He spent a week in Spain.

It is fun to camp in a green tent.

Milk is good for children's teeth.

I must not tramp on the flowers.

I can hear twigs snapping in the wind.

A drip from the tap drops in the sink.

I kept bumping into things in the dark.

The taps drip into the sink.

The frog jumps in the pond.

I must no stomp on the flowers.

A crab crept into a crack in the rock.

I kept bumping into things in the dark.

The clown did tricks with a chimpanzee.

The bench was cold and wet.

The champ swam thirteen laps in the pool.

The three girls wept.

The crab snaps at the fish.

What is that on the bookshelf?

The pram was under the tree.

The green croc went for a swim in the pond.

I like French food.

Phase Five Sentences

She can play the flute.

The boy came to the house to eat cake.

The girl saw a bluebird by the sea.

The boy came to the house to eat some pies.

The old dog took his bone home.

The crayons looked brand new.

She saw a bluebird by the sea.

An elephant stomped on the snake's tail.

The crayons looked new.

The old, grey house looks spooky and haunted.

My nose is running, and I must use a tissue.

I looked at the monkey's claws when it sat on the chimney.

The dog took his bone home.

Should you carry an elephant on your head?

Would you like to wave a magic wand?

Would you crawl into a thorn bush?

I like honey on my bagel.

I think the clouds look like puffs of smoke.

Mrs Blue makes cakes for Mr Yellow.

On Monday, mother will make the turkey for dinner.

I love beef jerky.

Phase Six Sentences

Grandad tried baling a wedding cake.

Father said, "The train's here early."

The mother went to the park and played with the puppies.

It is unusual to eat smelly cheese while walking in the park.

The space shuttle roared loudly as it took off.

The magician made the rabbit disappear in front of the girl's eyes.

There was a lot of excitement at the dance school's concert.

The wind blew strongly and knocked over a table.

Simon talked louder than Harry, and Joe was the loudest.

The teacher tested each child's spelling.

Jane flew a colourful kite over the white, frothy river.

The bride and groom were the luckiest couple on the island.

The eagle silently swooped down on its prey.

The dragon roared angrily at the brave, young knight.

The penniless girl wanted payment for the entertainment.

The boy's monthly disagreement with his parents started after he crashed his bicycle.

The reindeer fly over Santa's house annually.

The small, hairy gerbil carefully climbed up the metal cage.

I am unclear on the expectations.

The friendly children playfully threw chewy fruit cake at the Christmas elves.

My sister ate six boxes of crunchy, fresh Brazil nuts.

29
PRINTABLES
PHONEME STRIPS

BOGGLE BOARD

GLOSSARY

Abbreviation: A shortened form of a word with full stops indicating missing letters.

Accent: The way a language is pronounced.

Adjective: A word that describes a noun.

Adverb: A word that says how, when or where something happens.

Alliteration: Words that begin with the same sound alongside each other or close to each other in a sentence.

Apostrophe: A punctuation mark used to indicate possession or show where letters have been left out.

Auditory Discrimination: The ability to distinguish between different sounds in the environment.

Auditory Figure-Ground Discrimination: The ability to focus on important sounds in a noisy environment.

Auditory Memory: The ability to recall what has been heard.

Auditory Sequencing: The ability to recall words or sounds in order.

Bilateral Integration: The ability for the two hands to work together to perform a task, like holding a piece of paper with one hand while cutting with the other.

Blending: Joining sounds together to form a word.

Blog: An online journal or diary.

CCVC: Words made from a consonant, consonant, vowel, consonant. For example, frog.

Clause: A part of a sentence that contains a subject and a verb.

Collective noun: A word used to describe a group of animals or people.

Comma: A punctuation mark used to separate words or phrases in a sentence.

Command: A sentence that tells someone what to do.

Common Noun: Naming words for ordinary people, places, things, and ideas.

Compound Word: Two words joined together to form a new word.

Conjunction: A word used to connect phrases, words, or clauses in a sentence.

Consonant: All the letters of the alphabet, excluding the vowels.

Consonant Blends: Two or three consonants alongside each other in a word that makes two or three sounds.

Contraction: A word created by joining two words together and leaving out certain letters with an apostrophe to indicate the missing letters.

Co-ordinating Conjunction: A conjunction that joins two main clauses together in a sentence.

CVC: Words: words made from a consonant, vowel, consonant. For example, cat

CVCC: Words made from a consonant, vowel, consonant, consonant. For example, bend

Crossing the Midline: The ability to cross the invisible line that runs from the top of the head down through the middle of the body through the nose.

Decoding: This is the process whereby a child sees and can read a word.

Digraph: Two letters that make one sound.

Diphthong: A digraph where both vowel sounds are heard.

EHCP: Education, Health and Care Plan. This is a plan that is created in conjunction with the local council, it is for children who need more support and additional resources that the school lgenerally do not provide.

Exclamation: A sentence that expresses strong feelings.

Exclamation Mark: The punctuation mark used in an exclamation.

Expanded Noun Phrase: A phrase that consists of a noun and at least one adjective.

Graph: One letter representing one sound

Grapheme: A single letter or group of letters that represent one sound.

Hand dominance: The consistent use of one preferred hand for repetitive tasks.

Homographs: Words that are spelt the same but have different pronunciations and definitions.

Homophone: Words that sound the same but have different spellings and definitions.

IEP: Individualised Education Program/Plan. It is a plan set out by the teacher to support children who are still struggling after interventions have occurred and therefore need additional support.

Morpheme: The smallest complete part of a word.

Noun: A word for a person, place, thing, or idea.

Noun Phrase: A noun and the modifier that distinguishes the noun.

Object: The person, animal or thing referred to by the verb.

Object Manipulation: The ability to use tools like scissors, hairbrushes, and scissors effectively.

Onomatopoeia: Sounds used to mimic objects or animals.

Past tense: A sentence written about something that happened in the past.

Phoneme: A speech sound.

Phoneme Spotter: A worksheet or text containing the sound being taught or learnt.

Plural: Two or more animals, people, or things.

Polysyllabic words: words with more than one syllable.

Prefix: A beginning added on to a root word to change the meaning of the word.

Present tense: A sentence written about something that is happening now.

Pronoun: A word used in place of a noun.

Proper noun: A particular place, person, animal, thing, or idea. Proper nouns begin with capital letters.

Quadgraph: Four letters that make one sound.

Question: A sentence that asks for an answer.

Question mark: The punctuation that indicates the sentence is a question.

Rhyme: Words that have the same last sound.

Rhythm: The timing or beat in a word, sentence, or poem.

Root word: A whole word or part of a word onto which a prefix or suffix can be attached.

Schwa: A vowel sound 'uh.'

Segmenting: Breaking words into their separate sounds.

SEND: Special education needs and disability, children with specific health or educational needs.

Sensory Processing: The child's ability to interpret the messages he/she receives from their senses.

Sentence: A set of words together that form a complete idea, containing a subject and a verb.

Split digraph: Two letters represent one sound but are separated by a consonant; there are five split digraphs a-e, e-e, u-e, o-e, and i-e.

Statement: A sentence that states something.

Subordinating Conjunction: A conjunction that joins another phrase or clause onto the sentence to add extra information to the main clause.

Suffix: An ending added onto a root word.

Superlative: An adjective or adverb that suggests something is the most of, or the greatest/least of something.

Syllable: They sound like the beat in a word. You can count the syllables by clapping the beat of a word.

Tense: When an action takes place.

Trigraph: Three letters that make one sound.

Unvoiced: The airflow creates the sound.

Verb: A doing word.

Visual Attention: The ability to focus on the important information visually.

Visual Discrimination: The ability to see similarities and differences.

Visual Figure-Ground: The ability to find something on a busy background.

Visual Form Constancy: The understanding that a shape or letter remains the same despite its size or orientation.

Visual Memory: The ability to remember the shape of an object or the objects themselves.

Visual Sequential Memory: The ability to remember objects in order.

Visual Spatial Relationships: Understanding where things are in space and in relation to each other.

Voiced: This sound is made through friction.

Vowel: The letters a, e, i, o, and u and sometimes y

Word: A group of letters together that together have meaning.

REFERENCES

Insert Addy, L (2015) *Speed Up! A kinaesthetic programme to develop fluent handwriting*. UK: LDA.

Byrne, N, (2008) *LCP Phonics Planning, Day by Day Lesson Plans based on   Letters and Sounds*. LCP

Budden, Jo (2008) British Councill: Grouping Students, Available at: https://www.teachingenglish.org.uk/article/grouping-students (Accessed 15 May 2021)

(2021) Consortium the education supply people, Available at: https://www.consortiumeducation.com/ (Accessed: 10 April 2021).

Cripps, C. and Cox, R. (1996) *Joining the ABC*. Wisbech, Cambs: LDA

(2021) Dyslexia Reading Well, Available at:https://www.dyslexia-reading-well.com/support-files/the-44-phonemes-of-english.pdf (Accessed: 21 April 2021)

(2021) edu-k About Educational Kinesiology, Available at: https://braingym.org.uk/about-edu-k/ (Accessed: 7 April 2021)

(2021) Games Grown and Picked by Bananagrams. Available at: https://bananagrams.com/blogs/news/how-to-play-bananagrams-instructions-for-getting-started (Accessed: 17 March 2021)

(2021) Gov. uk, Department for Education. Available at: https://www.gov.uk/government/publications/phonics-teaching-materials-core-criteria-and-self-assessment/validation-of-systematic-synthetic-phonics-programmes-supporting-documentation (Accessed:20 May 2021)

(2021) 123 HomeSchool 4 Me Available at: https://www.123homeschool4me.com/kindergarten-word-family-sliders_24/ (Accessed: 21 March 2021)

Kelly, Melissa. (2020, August 27). Creating Effective Lesson Objectives. Retrieved https://www.thoughtco.com/lesson-objectives-that-produce-results-7763

(2021) Kid Sense: Visual Perception Available at: https://childdevelopment.com.au/areas-of-concern/visual-perception/ (Accessed 5 April 2021)

(2007) *Letters and Sounds: Principles and Practice of High-Quality Phonics, Six-phase Teaching Programme*. Department for Education and Skills

Lloyd, S. (1992) *The Phonics Handbook*. Chigwell: Jolly Learning Ltd.

Lundberg, I. Olofsson, A and Wall, S. (1980) Reading and Spelling Skills in the First School Years Predicted from Phonemic Awareness Skills in Kindergarten. *Scandinavian Journal of Psychology*, 21,159-173.

Masterson, J. Stuart, M. Dixon, M. &Lovejoy, S. (2003) Children's Printed Word Database. Economic and Social Research Council Funded Project, R00023406.

McGuinness, D. *Early Reading Instruction: What Science Really Tells Us About How to Teach Reading*

(2021) Mighty Writer, Available at: https://www.mightywriter.co.uk/ (Accessed: 11 April 2021)

(2021) Muse Printables, Available at: https://museprintables.com/c/writing-templates/category/animal/ (Accessed: 18 August 2021)

(2021) OxfordOwl, Available at: https://support.oxfordowl.co.uk/teacher-support/school-subscriptions/subscription-guidance/nelson-handwriting/ (Accessed 12 April 2021)

Parfetti, C. Beck, I. Bell, L and Hughes (1987) *Phonemic Knowledge and Learning to Read are Reciprocal: A Longitudinal   Study   of First Grade Children*. Merrill-Palmer Quarterly, 33,   283-39.

(2021) PhonicsPlay Available at: https://www.phonicsplay.co.uk/ (Accessed: 06 March 2021).

(2021) PuzzleMaker Discovery Education Available at https://www.puzzlemaker.discoveryeducation.com/ (Accessed: 3 May 2021)

(2021) Reading Elephant. Available at: https://www.readingelephant.com/phonics-books-overview/ (Accessed: 27 March 2021)

Rice, M. (1985) *Play Together Learn Together*. London: Rainbow Books

(2021) Sarah's Teaching Snippets Available at. https://sarahstilppets.com/phonemic-awareness-intervention-pack/ (Accessed 2 April 2021)

Share, D.L. Jorm, A.F. MacLean and Matthews, R (1984) Sources of Individual Differences in Reading Achievement. *Journal of Educational Psychology*, 76, 1309-1324r.

(2021) PhonicBooks, Available at: https://www.phonicbooks.co.uk/shop/ (Accessed: 19 May 2021)

(2021) Smart Kids, Available at: https://www.smartkids.co.uk/ (Accessed: 10 April 2021)

Strategies   for   Improving   Literacy   Skills   and   Students   with   CVI.

https://www.perkins.org/assets/downloads/webinars/presentation/strategies-for-improving-literacy.pdf

(2021) Start Here Parenting, Available at: https://startthereparents.com/dysgraphia-symptoms/ (Accessed 10 May 2021).

(2021) https://www.flickr.com/photos/whiteafrican/731467843

(2021) Sweet Clip Art, Available at: https://sweetclipart.com/ (Acessesed:8 April 2021)

(2021) Talk for Writing, Available at: https://www.talk4writing.com/ (Accessed: 15 May 2021)

(2021) The Anonymous OT Available at: https://theanonymousot.com/2018/07/05/10-go-to-games- to-work-on-visual-perception/ (Accessed 9 April 2021)

(2021) Teacher's Takeout Available at: http://www.teacherstakeout.com/2015/02/44-sounds-of-english-language-freebie.html?m=1 (Accessed 27 March 2021).

(2021) Teach with Laughter, Available at: https://teachwithlaughter.blogspot.com/2017/08/reading-strategies.html (Accessed: 13 May 2021)

(2021) Teroes, Available at: https://www.teroes.com/2019/03/what-is-dyspraxia.html (Accessed 14 May 2021)

(2021) The THRASSinstitute Available at: https://www.thrass.com.au/ (Accessed 06 March 2021).

(2013) *The 2014 Primary National Curriculum in England, Key Stages 1&2Framework Document.* Shurville Publishing.

(2021) The Tricky Word Song Available at: https://www.youtube.com/watch?v=TvMyssfAUx0 (Accessed: 06 March 2021)

(2021) Twinkl, Available at: https://www.twinkl.co.uk/blog/plenary-ideas (Accessed: 15 May 2021)

(2021) Understood, Available at: https://www.understood.org/en/learning-thinking-differences/child-learning-disabilities/dysgraphia/difference-between-dysgraphia-dyspraxia (Accessed at 14 May 2021)

(2021) Welcome to MyCuteGraphics! Available at: https://www.mycutegraphics.com/ (Accessed:06 March 2021).

Wernham, S. Lloyd, S. (2010) *Phonics Teacher's Book.* Chigwell: Jolly Learning Ltd (2021) https://www.flickr.com/photos/pennuja/5931765266

(2021) Wiki How to do anything. How to Play Boggle. Available at: https://www.wikihow.com/Play-Boggle#:~:text=%Two0Setting%Two0Up%Two0%Two0One%Two0Put%Two0the%Two0game,run%Two0out%Two0of%Two0sand%Two0in%Two0three...%Two0More%Two0 (Accessed 07 March 2021)

PICTURE ACKNOWLEDGEMENTS

(2021) https://en.wikipedia.org/wiki/Charcoal (art). By Stephhzz - Own work, CC BY-SA 3.0, https://commons.wikimedia.org/w/index.php?curid=11728347

(2021) Free Kindergarten Teacher and Parent Resources. https://www.kindergartenteacherresources.com/spot-difference/ (Accessed 5 May 2021)

(2021) Marco Verch. https://foto.wuestenigel.com/jenga-tower-game-with-wooden-blocks-on-white-background/

(2021) Free images Live https://www.freeimageslive.co.uk/free_stock_image/colorful-bricks-jpg

(2021) By Original image by Whitney Waller, red lines added - connect-the-dots, CC BY-SA 2.0, https://commons.wikimedia.org/w/index.php?curid=45762476

(2021) By Maciozik - Own work, CC BY-SA 3.0, https://commons.wikimedia.org/w/index.php?curid=19732202

(2021) By Maciozik - Own work, CC BY-SA 3.0, https://commons.wikimedia.org/w/index.php?curid=19732202

(2021) By Udjat - Own work, CC BY-SA 3.0, https://commons.wikimedia.org/w/index.php?curid=10576717

(2021) By No machine-readable author provided. Peng assumed (based on copyright claims). - No machine-readable source provided. Own work assumed (based on copyright claims)., CC BY-SA 3.0, https://commons.wikimedia.org/w/index.php?curid=27659

(2021) By Michael Rivera - Own work, CC BY-SA 3.0, https://commons.wikimedia.org/w/index.php?curid=23824885

(2021) By Shritwod - Own work, CC0, https://commons.wikimedia.org/w/index.php?curid=74999741

By Nevit Dilmen - Own work, CC BY-SA 3.0, https://commons.wikimedia.org/w/index.php?curid=3775216

By Nevit Dilmen - Own work, CC BY-SA 3.0, https://commons.wikimedia.org/w/index.php?curid=3775221

(2021) By Mokkie - Own work, CC BY-SA 4.0, https://commons.wikimedia.org/w/index.php?curid=45119586

By Jim Pennucci from Hope, USA - Painting, CC BY 2.0, https://commons.wikimedia.org/w/index.php?curid=19451952

By Sue Clark - Flickr: Jack and Jill, Public Domain, https://commons.wikimedia.org/w/index.php?curid=16141467

By Tim Pierce - originally posted to Flickr as lost, CC BY 2.0, https://commons.wikimedia.org/w/index.php?curid=4614902

(2021) File: Two monks tangram paradox.svg. https://en.wikipedia.org/wiki/File:Two_monks_tangram_paradox.svg

<a href="https://www.vecteezy.com/free-photos">Free Stock photos by Vecteezy</a>

ABOUT THE AUTHOR

Kerry Dickinson has been teaching for more than twenty years in private and public schools both in the UK and overseas. She studied Primary School Teaching, Early Years Education and English Literature and Language. She has worked in EYFS, Keystage 1 and Keystage 2 and has an excellent grasp of the English Curriculum.

As a child Kerry was touched by how hard it was for some children to learn to read, write and spell. This fascination later developed into a passion that fuelled endless hours of research and study as she tried to find ways to help pupils overcome difficulties and develop a love of language. Later when Kerry started working with student teachers and parents. She felt moved to share her knowledge with others and a short blog post soon developed into a book.

Printed in Great Britain
by Amazon

23862473R00064